The Cultural Politics of Slam Poetry

The Cultural Politics of Slam Poetry

Race, Identity, and the Performance of Popular Verse in America

Susan B. A. Somers-Willett

THE UNIVERSITY OF MICHIGAN PRESS / Ann Arbor

2012   2011   2010   2009   4   3   2   1

A CIP catalog record for this book is available from the British Library.

Library of Congress Cataloging-in-Publication Data

Somers-Willett, Susan B. A., 1973–
    The cultural politics of slam poetry : race, identity, and the
performance of popular verse in America / Susan B. A. Somers-
Willett.
        p.   cm.
    Includes bibliographical references and index.
    ISBN-13: 978-0-472-07059-6 (cloth : alk. paper)
    ISBN-10: 0-472-07059-2 (cloth : alk. paper)
    ISBN-13: 978-0-472-05059-8 (pbk. : alk. paper)
    ISBN-10: 0-472-05059-1 (pbk. : alk. paper)
    1. Performance poetry—United States—History and criticism.
2. American poetry—20th century—History and criticism.   3. Race in
literature.   4. Identity (Psychology) in literature.   5. Oral
interpretation of poetry.   6. Poetry slams—United States—History.
7. Poetry—Political aspects—United States.   I. Title.
PN4151.S67   2009
808.5'45—dc22   2009004564

For my slam family

Because Slam is unfair.

Because Slam is too much fun.

Because poetry.

Because rules.

Because poetry rules.

Because the poetry gets lost.

Because poetry is an endangered species Slam finds and revivifies.

Because you cannot reduce a poem to its numerological equivalent.

Because hey it's poetry in everyday life every Sunday at 7:30 PM.

Because I can do that.

> **—Bob Holman, from "Praise Poem for Slam: Why Slam Causes Pain and Is a Good Thing"**

Acknowledgments

Several colleagues helped make this project possible. I first must give thanks to my friend and mentor Kurt Heinzelman, who read this project at every stage and supplied expert guidance, delivered careful critique, and displayed unflagging enthusiasm for this book. To my teachers and colleagues Sabrina Barton, Matti Bunzl, Mia Carter, Shelley Fisher Fishkin, Paul Gray, Joni Jones, Doug Taylor, and Stacy Wolf, thank you for encouraging my interdisciplinary approaches to scholarship.

I am also indebted to the institutions at which work on this project took place, the University of Texas at Austin, the University of Illinois at Urbana-Champaign, and Carnegie Mellon University. I owe a debt of gratitude to the Harry Ransom Humanities Research Center for the use of its facilities and access to its minstrel show collection. A very special thanks is extended to Nicolette Schneider and Rick Watson in the Performing Arts Division for their assistance with that collection. I also thank the students of my Poetry and Performance course at the University of Illinois for sharing their ideas about poetry and hip-hop with me.

This book has benefited from careful readings by members of the National Poetry Slam community. To Cristin O'Keefe Aptowicz, Greg Gilliam, Jeremy Richards, and Scott Woods, thank you for your comments, suggestions, and comradeship. I would also like to acknowledge the host of slam artists who made this project possible. Thanks to Krystal Ashe, Tara Betts, Roger Bonair-Agard, Michael Brown, Staceyann Chin, Corey Cokes, Steve Colman, Black Ice, Gayle Danley, Paul Devlin, Mark Eleveld, Mayda del Valle, Ragan Fox, Flowmentalz, Bruce George, Georgia Me, Regie Gibson, Gary Mex Glazner, Guy LeCharles Gonzalez, Mike Henry, Bob Holman, Jean Howard, Tyehimba Jess, Liz Jones, Lisa King, Marc Levin, Taylor Mali, Steve Marsh, Jack McCarthy, Jeffrey McDaniel, Ray McNiece, Amalia Ortiz, Alix Olson, Eirik Ott, Lynne Procope, Jerry Quickley, Sonya Renee, Rives, Louis Rodriguez, Shappy Seasholtz, Sekou tha Misfit, Beau Sia, Marc Smith, Patricia Smith, Phil

West, Saul Williams, Allan Wolf, and Genevieve Van Cleve for their words and work. A huge thanks to Poetry Slam, Incorporated, for supporting me as both a poet and a scholar. I also owe a large debt to all of the members of the national slam community for sharing their poetry, opinions, and hotel rooms with me over the last dozen years. Thank you, slam family, for embracing and challenging me and ensuring that my scholarly pursuits were never the least bit soporific.

LeAnn Fields, my editor, believed in the possibilities of this book from the very start and displayed patience and finesse in its editing. Great thanks to her, the copyediting team, and everyone else at the University of Michigan Press for ensuring that this book was published with enthusiasm and care.

I am finally and most greatly indebted to the organizations that funded this project at various stages. I am deeply grateful for the support of an Andrew W. Mellon Foundation Postdoctoral Fellowship and an American Association of University Women American Fellowship, both of which made writing this book possible. I also thank the Center for the Arts in Society at Carnegie Mellon University and the Hedgebrook Retreat for Women Writers for their generous support during the editing of this book.

Little can be said to adequately express the many ways my family has supported me over the years. To my husband, Ernie Cline, thank you for your technical support, encouragement, and willingness to make treks across the country with me to ensure the success of this project. Meeting you was the best thing that could have happened to me at a poetry slam. My mother, Patricia Somers, supplied more support throughout my young career than any other single person. Thank you for every day of it.

I also extend gratitude to the editors of the journals in which portions of this project were previously published in earlier forms. Portions of chapter 3 were published in the *Journal of the Midwestern Modern Language Association* as "Slam Poetry and the Cultural Politics of Performing Identity" (spring 2005). Portions of chapter 4 were published in the *Iowa Journal of Cultural Studies* as "Def Poetry's Public: Spoken Word Poetry and the Racial Politics of Going Mainstream" (spring 2006) and in the *Text, Practice, Performance Journal of Cultural Studies* as "'Representing' Slam Poetry: Ambivalence, Gender, and Black Authenticity in *Slam*" (spring 2002). Small portions of the epilogue were published in *RATTLE* as "Can Slam Poetry Matter?" (summer 2007).

Grateful acknowledgment is made to the following publishers, authors, and organizations: Tara Betts for permission to reprint an excerpt from her poem, "Rock 'n' Roll Be a Black Woman"; Roger Bonair-Agard for permission to reprint his poem, "How Do We Spell Freedom"; Staceyann Chin for permission to reprint excerpts from her poem, "I Don't Want to Slam"; The Harry Ransom Humanities Research Center at The University of Texas at Austin for permission to reprint the Virginia Minstrels woodcuts, promotional material for the Simmons & Slocums Minstrel Company, and the "Poet" sketch from *The Boys of New York End Men's Joke Book* from their Minstrel Show Collection; Lionsgate Films for permission to reproduce the cover art from the DVD of *Slam* (1998, dir. Marc Levin); Taylor Mali for permission to reprint his poem, "How to Write a Political Poem"; Poetry Slam, Incorporated, for permission to reprint "The Official Rules of National Poetry Slam Competition" and "The Official National Poetry Slam 'Emcee Spiel'" from *The Official 2007 Poetry Slam Rulebook* and "The Official National Poetry Slam Instructions for Judges" from the 2007 National Poetry Slam Judge's Scoring instructions; and Genevieve Van Cleve for permission to reprint an excerpt from her poem, "I Was the Worst Feminist in the World."

Contents

Introduction

Slam and the Search for Poetry's Great Audience

To have great poets, there must be great audiences, too.
—Walt Whitman, "Ventures, on an Old Theme," 1892

Anyone who hopes to broaden poetry's audience—critic, teacher, librarian, poet, or lonely literary amateur—faces a daunting challenge. How does one persuade justly skeptical readers, in terms they can understand and appreciate, that poetry still matters?
—Dana Gioia, "Can Poetry Matter?" 1992

On or about August 1988, contemporary American poetry changed. The relations between poetry and its audience—between academics and their venerated tomes, MFA students and their assigned readings, rappers and the rhymes they busted—shifted. The catalyst for this shift was the claim that poetry and the intellectual culture it inspired was dead.

In August 1988, *Commentary* published Joseph Epstein's editorial "Who Killed Poetry?" which made the familiar claim that poetry was rarely enjoyed outside of a small subculture of readers. The cause for this "vacuum," Epstein posited, was the vast and growing number of academic creative writing programs in the United States and the poets firmly ensconced there as teachers.[1] The following year, the *Writer's Chronicle,* a trade magazine published by the Association of Writers and Writing Programs, reprinted Epstein's essay along with responses from 101 writers over the span of three issues. One of those writers was the poet-critic Dana Gioia (now chairman of the National Endowment for the Arts), who published an extended version of this response entitled "Can Poetry Matter?" in the April 1991 *Atlantic*. He collected this and other essays about poetry in an eponymous book in 1992.

In this title essay, Gioia furthered Epstein's argument, claiming that Americans lived within a "divided literary culture," one that had a "superabundance of poetry within a small class and [an] impoverishment outside it. One might even say that outside the classroom—where society demands that the two groups interact—poets and the common reader are no longer on speaking terms." Poetry, he argued, had lost its larger nonacademic audience, which "cut across lines of race, class, age, and occupation" and was "poetry's bridge to the general culture." Gioia placed the onus of poetry's subcultural status on poets who had abandoned working-class bohemia for academic careers.[2] The dire situation of verse was only to be remedied, he argued, by seeking an audience for poetry outside of the academy.

The volume of responses to Gioia's essay was overwhelming—the *Atlantic* received more letters about it than any other article in decades. Reactions were also severe—especially, as one might expect, from poets teaching in academic writing programs. The essay's popularity inspired a wave of criticism for those waging the debate as well. Donald Hall's 1989 essay in *Harper's* magazine, "Death to the Death of Poetry," accused poets of such navel gazing: "While most readers and poets agree that 'nobody reads poetry'—and we warm ourselves by the gregarious fires of our solitary art—maybe a multitude of nobodies assembles the great audience Whitman looked for."[3] Similarly, the poet Richard Tillinghast speculated in the *Writer's Chronicle,* "Perhaps the crisis of confidence among poets, the unseemly hand-wringing, reveals that many of us really are afflicted with Nielsen Ratings syndrome, that we are not writing for the work's sake but from a desire to be noticed."[4]

Both authors were quite right. In essence, what these critics debated was not the state or quality of poetry itself but the urgency with which poetry needed to seek public attention. Without a relationship with popular audiences—or at the very least a relationship with a small intelligentsia outside of the academy—poetry, Gioia and others claimed, was doomed to a dinosaur's fate. Engaging a classic tension between the academy and the public and the verse produced within these spheres, the argument was a fresh iteration of what Walt Whitman had been concerned with a century earlier: finding poetry's great audience. Part of this resurgence of interest in poetry's popularity resulted in anthologies such as *The Best American Poetry* series edited by David Lehman, which was itself initiated in 1988. The concern for poetry's livelihood carried on through the 1990s. In 1996, the Academy of American Poets—a long-standing nonprofit organization supporting American poets and poetry—proclaimed April National Poetry Month. One of its first projects was to hand out thousands of copies of T. S. Eliot's *The Waste Land* to those in line at the Houston post office on tax day (because

April *is* the cruelest month). For the first time in decades, revitalized interest bloomed not just in poetry but in the audience for poetry. Poets and critics openly asked, "Who is reading poetry? For whom is it being written? Has poetry's spirit of necessity and urgency died—not for its practitioners but for its readers?" At once, American poets began to investigate the relationships poetry had with the American people with renewed zeal.

In the midst of these years of artistic anxiety, Marc Smith, a white Chicago construction worker turned poet, tested another venue for verse that sought an audience outside of the sanctioned space of the academy. Smith had attended readings where performances consisted "mostly of poets reading to poets. . . . If you ever wanted to read your poetry anywhere, almost always an academic set it up."[5] To boot, Smith remarks, attendance at these readings was almost always poor and audiences tended to view such events with disdain. "I knew that the public scorn for poetry readings was an outcome of how it was being presented: a lifeless monotone that droned on and on with no consideration for the structure or the pacing of the event—let the words do the work, the poets would declare, mumbling to a dribble of friends, wondering why no one else had come to listen."[6] Setting his sights on larger popular audiences for poetry, Smith turned to the bars and cabarets of Chicago's white, working-class neighborhoods.

In collaboration with other local artists, Smith instigated a wild variety show of Dadaist poetry, cabaret, musical experimentation, and performance art—all performed in blue-collar venues where locals were usually looking to watch a game over a couple of brews. The result was incongruous to say the least. The performance artist Jean Howard described this early performance poetry scene as barely controlled chaos in an audience of Joe six-packs.

> One of the earliest, most primitive nightspots was the Get Me High Lounge located in a north side, blue collar Chicago neighborhood. This small, dark, graffiti-walled bar offered a stage with the bathroom located in the back, so patrons had to walk on stage during performances to gain access to it. Marc Smith had secured Monday nights, a traditionally dead night at the bar, to showcase the handful of poets exploring performance art. Local neighborhood patrons trying to watch a Cubs game and down a beer would find themselves being assaulted by poets utilizing wild gestures,

musical instruments, boom boxes, costuming, and theatrical makeup.[7]

Smith, who also organized performances at the Déjà Vu and Green Mill Bars, experimented with many modes of performance in tandem with his poetry, including vaudeville, ensemble work, and open mic readings. In the summer of 1986, when he ran out of material to complete a set during an ensemble show at the Green Mill, Smith stumbled on a format that stuck. He held a mock competition in the show's final set, letting the audience judge the poems performed onstage—first with boos and applause and later with numeric scores.[8] The audience was compelled by this format and Smith soon made the competition a regular attraction on Sunday nights at the Green Mill. It was there, among the clinking tumblers of whiskey and wafts of cigarette smoke, that the Uptown Poetry Slam was born.

It was more than fortuitous that while Gioia and Hall were duking it out over poetry's audience in the *Atlantic* and *Harper's* Smith found a nontraditional audience for poetry in Chicago's working-class barrooms. Slam poets' frustration over the academic monopoly on poetry readings and the attending highbrow airs of these events helped fuel a rowdy, countercultural atmosphere at slams, one that persists at many venues today. Audiences at the Green Mill were and are encouraged to boo or applaud the poet onstage, a far cry from the quiet attentiveness expected of audiences at the typical poetry reading. With the usual expectations of reverence and silence thrown out the window, a different type of relationship between poets and audiences became possible at a slam—one that was highly interactive, theatrical, physical, and immediate. "The traditional stagnant reading of a poem was no match for the level of audience engagement possible when poetry was presented as a physical/full sensory experience," Howard remarks. "For a few experimenting poets, like myself, there was no turning back."[9]

The poetry slam soon gained loyal followings beyond Chicago. Poets and fans spread the contest to other urban centers such as San Francisco and New York, meriting the first National Poetry Slam (NPS) in 1990 with poets from each of these cities. Since then, the slam has experienced exponential growth. Poetry slams now attract audiences not only in metropolitan cities but also in places as distant as Sweden and the United Kingdom or as remote as Fargo, North Dakota, and Anchorage, Alaska. They are held in bars, bookstores, coffeehouses, and theaters. Today, the National Poetry Slam hosts teams from over seventy cities across the United States, Canada, and France, and a nonprofit organization, Poetry Slam, Incorporated (PSI), was formed to oversee the competition and enforce its rules. The competition has become so popular that a waiting list is necessary to accommodate teams wanting to participate. Other national competitions have surfaced under PSI's governance: the Individual World Poetry Slam (iWPS) and the Women of the World Poetry Slam.[10] With slams surfacing in the vast majority of American states and slam poets performing their work in feature films, in documentaries, on cable television, and on Broadway, the slam is a phenomenon that appears to have captured our national imagination. In 2004, slam poetry even garnered the dubious honor of becoming the subject of a book in the Complete Idiot's Guide series coauthored by Marc Smith himself.[11]

In addition to fostering a countercultural atmosphere and disseminating poetry in unconventional venues, the slam has thrived through the exercise of certain democratic ideals meant to contrast with exclusive academic conventions. Slams are rowdy yet welcoming events on the whole. From its beginnings, the poetry slam has adopted an open-door policy: anyone can sign up to slam, and anyone in the audience is qualified to judge. This, of course, also means that there is usually great variety in the quality of the work performed at slams. A visit to one's own local poetry slam will most likely entail witnessing a mix of impressive and trite poems delivered both as powerfully or poorly. As the event progresses, poets are eliminated and rewarded based on the judges' scores—effectively putting the audience in the seat of critical power. Such an emphasis on the audience as critic stands apart from more traditional readings that celebrate or revere authors already deemed worthy by literary authorities. The poetry slam was founded on the tenets that the audience is not obligated to listen to the poet, that the poet should compel the audience to listen to him or her, that anyone may judge a competition, and that the competition should be open to all people and all forms of poetry.[12] Slam poetry is verse to which, at least theoretically, anyone can have access and whose worth anyone can determine. The accessibility of slam poetry is facilitated and perhaps demanded by the medium of performance, which is bounded by time, space, and—perhaps most important—an audience's attention span. In nationally certified slam competitions, poems are limited to an approximate three-minute window, which poet and showman Bob Holman notes is the length of a pop song.[13] The main motivation for this time limit was to keep certified slams within reasonable time frames, as audiences were proving restless during competitions that lasted longer than a couple of hours.

Poetry slams, because of their dedication to accessibility and increasing the numbers of poetry practitioners and fans outside of the academy, appeared to be a tailor-made solution to Epstein's and Gioia's trouble with contemporary poetry. Poetry slams deliberately took verse outside of the academy, taking evaluative power away from academic critics and giving it to popular audiences. In a recent essay, Gioia calls performance poetry's reemergence into popular culture "without a doubt the most surprising and significant development in recent American poetry."[14] The combined practices of poetry slams, rap performances, and other types of poetry transmitted and consumed through performance have, he argues, been the primary forces leading poetry into the twenty-first century, in large part igniting the renaissance contemporary American poetry is currently enjoying.

Perhaps most surprising is that this renaissance is being celebrated particularly by American youth, one of poetry's most unlikely audiences twenty years ago. Indeed, poetry in performance has become so popular in youth culture that verse has penetrated mainstream commercial markets, finding its way into McDonald's advertisements, Partnership for a Drug-Free America public service announcements, *MTV News,* and episodes of *The Simpsons.* In the music industry, some socially conscious hip-hop artists are now rebranding themselves as spoken word poets, whereas twenty years ago the title was, as rapper LL Cool J put it, "financial poison" for a hip-hop artist's career.[15] These examples suggest that America is in the midst of an explosion of verse in popular culture, one facilitated by the performance of poetry in live and recorded media but, like hip-hop, one also facilitated by expressions of identity, particularly of race and class.

Slam's emphases on diversity, inclusion, and democracy have resulted in a "pluralism" among its poets; on the national level, slammers hold a bevy of readings outside of the national competition celebrating marginalized racial, sexual, and gender identities. Such pluralism, the scholar Tyler Hoffman remarks, "points to the fact that the spoken word in the U.S. in recent decades is tied up in powerful social movements that reframed—and validated—cultural identities of minorities."[16] Slam's openness to all people and all types of poetry suggests a specific political inquiry in its practice, one that slam poets make explicit in their work about identity: a challenge to the relative lack of diversity they feel is represented in the academy, the canon, and dominant culture. For many of these poets, the debate over poetry's popularity was not only about the survival of the genre in the public sphere but also about how poetry reflected cultural privilege and institutional power. In slams, poets rallied against the literary canon's lack of diversity. Poets in the film *Slamnation* describe the poetry slam as "a representative democracy," a "level playing field" in which equal access is granted to those denied more traditional poetic recognition such as publication by esteemed presses and participation in academic writing communities.[17] In the 2007 NPS *Poet's Guide,* slam champion Roger Bonair-Agard remarks, "We know 'canon' is narrow-minded and for all its beauty needs to be sacked and overturned if it is to be made more expansive."[18] Poet Jeffrey McDaniel comments that to slam poets "don't need a degree or a letter of recommendation, which is why the slam community is far more multicultural than the academy."[19] These poets suggest that the popularity of slam poetry has meaning beyond the spheres of literature and performance, yielding cultural and political ramifications. As it explores the political possibilities of identity, slam poetry begs to be regarded not only as a performance poetry movement but also—as Marc Smith once suggested—as a social movement.[20]

Slam's commitment to plurality and diversity has led slam poets to linger on personal and political themes, the most common of them being the expression of marginalized identity. The vast majority of work performed at poetry slams is an expression of the poets' identities; these recent trends compelled one veteran poet from its ranks, Genevieve Van Cleve, to call slam poetry "an art of self-proclamation."[21] The poetry rewarded at slams has been praised as a more "authentic" variety of verse by many sources, including the poets themselves. "Vague as it may sound," Maria Damon writes,

> the criterion for slam success seems to be some kind of "realness"—authenticity at the physical/sonic and metaphysical/emotional-intellectual-spiritual levels. This is why close listening is crucial; you're not just listening for technique, or "original imagery," or raw emotion, but for some transmission/recognition of resonant difference . . . a gestalt that effects a "felt change of consciousness" on the part of the listener.[22]

Damon's description suggests that the practice of rewarding performances for their "authenticity" or the "transmission of resonant difference" is a performative effect (as opposed to a textual effect). If Damon
is correct, then, in the case of slam poetry about identity, reward stems
not just from the expression of marginalized identity but from the way
that identity is performed onstage. That is, poems deemed the most authentic by slam audiences depend at least in part on the complex dynamics of identity exchanged between poets and audiences. Considering that of the fifteen individual champions of the National Poetry Slam
all but six have been African American, this practice also seems to pose
specific questions about authenticity and marginalized identity.

The overarching questions compelling this project are those of how
and why marginalized voices—and in particular African American
voices—are received as more authentic or real than other voices at poetry slams. Slams are places where all types of marginalized identities
are celebrated and expressed, and yet when it comes to rewarding these
expressions those of black identity are consistently more rewarded by
audiences at the national level. Exactly why this dynamic exists is at
the heart of this project, for it reveals not only how identity is performed and received at a slam but how identity can operate in American culture.

The identities expressed by slam poets are performative—that is,
they are performed consciously or unconsciously for audiences to certain ends. Because identity is an effect of performance in the world, just
as it is at a poetry slam, what is authentic about identity is not the realness or truth it is often used to connote but the repetition and reception
of certain behaviors and characteristics over time. That is, what is often
deemed authentic by an audience is actually a norm of tried identity
behavior. Poetry slams, as laboratories for identity expression and performance, present unique opportunities to witness this exchange between poet and audience in action. Slams prove cultural stages where
poets perform identities and their audiences confirm or deny them as
"authentic" via scoring.

This is not to say that authenticity does not exist, only to say that authenticity exists as a performance in which a subject and his or her audience agree that an identity is successfully and convincingly portrayed. It is when we forget that authenticity is such a
performance—when, at a poetry slam, authenticity and marginalized
identity are equated without keeping in mind the performative dynam-

ics of such an exchange—that it can prove problematic. This is most likely to occur in the commercial genre of spoken word poetry (which I separate from slam poetry because of its noncompetitive and commercial focus), where poets of color are often marketed to young multiethnic and white middle-class audiences, sometimes in ghettocentric ways. Still, there is also room for political activism in such an exchange, especially when parody or a persona is used to investigate identity in critical ways, and so even commercial venues for performance poetry can be places of serious thought and change. Socially conscious poets know they must skillfully negotiate their participation in commercial ventures, and debate within the slam community has been waged for years about the pros and cons of "selling out" to reach mainstream audiences.

Acknowledging that what passes as authentic behavior is a symptom of larger systems of meaning and power does not mean that identities performed at slams are doomed to confirm the status quo. Rather, as places where identities are newly authenticated, poetry slams are places of possibility, insight, and connection. They are places where the possibilities of identity are explored, and their study contributes understandings about the complex interactions and desires between poets and their audiences. Instead of being windows on culture, poetry slams *are* culture; they are places where interracial exchanges are made and marginalized identities are invented, reflected, affirmed, and refigured.

Of course, there is some contention within the slam community about whether or not one can refer to "slam poetry" at all; some embrace the mantle while others deny that slam is any different from other types of poetry. The key to understanding slam poetry as a body of work has little to do with form or style. Instead, because a range of forms, tones, and modes of address exist in slam practice, such poetry is best understood by what it means to achieve or effect: a more intimate and authentic connection to its audience. To do this, slam poetry aims to entertain its audience and be competitive yet inventive within the structure of official rules. Because these rules dictate that the performer of a slam poem must also be its author, authorship itself becomes a self-conscious performance at a slam, achieving a hyperawareness of self and identity. In their focus on celebrating diversity and liberal politics, slam aesthetics frequently correspond to performing marginalized identity in order to engage (and at times exploit) a slam audience's shared value of difference. Because local slam venues vary so much in tenor and audience, I limit my discussion here to poetry performed at the national level of competition and in nationally distributed media. For the same reason, I selected the poets and poems represented in this book for their iconic status within the NPS and spoken word communities. Almost all of the poems here have been performed on at least one NPS finals stage, and many of the poets are national champions. Limiting my discussion to the national context can, I believe, give a broader perspective on how slam poetry engages the cultural politics of difference in America even as it may give short shrift to the more unique aspects of local communities.[23]

This book is informed by my position as someone who has, for more than a decade, participated in the National Poetry Slam community as a competitor, team member, coach, volunteer, and audience member. As a participant-observer, witnessing the slam grow and change over time has allowed me unique access to the strategies slam poets use in competition and the challenges they (we) face as the slam has gained the national spotlight. My experiences in the national slam community have no doubt influenced my analysis here, as have my own poetic and performative sensibilities. As a participant who has seen reporters reductively praise the slam for its "fresh urban vibe" and an equal number of critics pan it for its "ranting pedanticism," I have longed for a more accurate, serious, and nuanced picture of what slam poets do and how their audiences receive them. My response is this book.

I am also acutely aware of my position as a white woman writing a book that takes a critical look at performances of race. Rather than be hindered by my position—or worse, rendering it invisible—I write with it at the forefront of my mind. Although I acknowledge that I do not have access to all of the personal experiences of my diverse subjects, I believe that investigating the interactions between poets of color and white, middle-class audiences (and by proxy my own subject position) is of great value. The performance of identity across race and class divides poses both possibilities and limitations for slam poets, and I wish to consider all of the pros and cons of performing these identities in competitive and commercial contexts, even as they may trouble my own roles as a poet, performer, and scholarly interlocutor.

Slam poetry, using the cultural rubrics of race and identity, has undeniably and fundamentally changed the relationship between American popular audiences and poetry; in tandem with other popular manifestations of the lyric in mass media such as hip-hop and spoken word, one could even argue that it has broken that relationship wide open. Still, this project does not intend to be a celebration of slam poetry's popularity, nor does it attempt to defend slam poetry from its critics. Rather, it is concerned with what slam poetry's reception can tell us about race and identity in American culture and how poetry slams encourage popular audiences to seek a broader relationship with American verse. I consider myself neither a champion of the slam genre nor a detractor of it but rather a poet who is interested in how performance can inform her writing and a critic interested in how poetry slams generate new avenues of public discourse for poets and audiences. As a writer who wears the many hats of slam poet, academic poet, critic, and scholar, I hope the perspective of my experience proves enlightening not limiting.

In focusing on the reception of African American slam poets and the ideas of blackness and authenticity that circulate in performance poetry, I do not intend to frame the slam as an entirely black phenomenon, nor do I mean to give undue stress to racial difference in slam poetry. Rather, I mean to reflect the overwhelming attention that marginalized identity in general and racial difference in particular are given in slam circles. Although slam poetry is open to and includes people of all cultural orientations and persuasions, the focus is often on poets of color, working-class poets, women, and other culturally marginalized groups. This focus reflects, I believe, a more general trend in contemporary American poetry toward recognizing and nurturing more authors of traditionally marginalized social groups (in some places almost exclusively). Some may argue that this trend has gone too far, making political correctness the ruler of poetic taste, while others may feel it has not gone far enough, signaling a sincere wish for the inclusion of diverse voices. I believe that both desires operate consciously or unconsciously among critics, writers, and audiences of poetry and that both sentiments are important to the kind of intercultural exchange that can happen in venues such as poetry slams. The fact remains that, for better or worse, audiences of poetry today are being exposed to many more nonwhite, nontraditional voices than they ever have before, and at poetry slams that difference is celebrated and rewarded.

The National Poetry Slam community is at a crucial juncture at this time as its artists and organizers decide individually and collectively how to negotiate mainstream interest in the genre. For some poets, touring on the college circuit, recording spoken word albums, and making mainstream media appearances are ultimate career goals. Others prefer performing at and organizing poetry slams in their local communities. Although many poets agree that the slam should persist and grow, they are divided about how to negotiate the commercial interests that come with such growth. Currently, Poetry Slam, Incorporated has discouraged widespread commercial involvement with the National Poetry Slam, and commercial ventures such as *Russell Simmons Presents Def Poetry* have begun to flourish outside of the NPS community. Enterprising poet-performers, however, are starting to skate between the competitive (slam) and commercial (spoken word) arenas, and the market continues to broaden for versifiers billing themselves as spoken word poets. Although the term *spoken word poetry* can be used to designate a number of different types of verse, in this book I use it to connote performance poetry through which one can witness competing commercial and artistic interests, especially as they play out in contemporary media and through associations with hip-hop culture.

As it has grown, the slam has seen an infusion of hip-hop-inspired performance, so much so that newcomers may mistakenly assume that the competition grew out of African American hip-hop culture as opposed to its white, working-class roots. Still, even when considering this history and the vast range of poetry performed at slams, it is clear that hip-hop is an important influence on many slam poets today. Poets commonly employ the hip-hop idiom on the slam stage, and some of them use the same material in both ciphers and slams. Slam poetry and hip-hop also engage similar issues of authenticity and identity, especially as they intersect with African American cultural production and address a call to "realness." The popularity of hip-hop music and culture has helped funnel poets and audiences into the slam, and this may be one reason why African American identity is so often articulated and rewarded on the national slam scene. However, the complex exchange of desires between slam poets and audiences are more than the product of hip-hop's influence. The preponderance of and anxieties over black expression in slam suggests a pattern of identity performance and reception—especially as it occurs between African American artists and white, middle-class audiences—that is at the foundation of American popular culture.

Among slam poets, it is generally agreed that one's involvement with poetry slams, at least as a competitor, has a shelf life. Although some veteran poets have competed in the NPS over several years, most poets leave the competitive arena after one or two years on national teams. However, most also continue their pursuits in poetry and performance. The slam has proven a laboratory for a new generation of artists fusing genres who are now finding success in American theater, literature, music, and the academy. Some slam poets, like Saul Williams or Sage Francis, move on to become recording artists, fusing hip-hop and music in new ways. Others, like Mayda del Valle and Roger Bonair-Agard, go on to perform one-person shows that grow from their slam material. Still more enroll in prestigious MFA programs after their tenure in the slam community, and others, like this author, pursue scholarship in the fields of English or theater. Some go on to publish their poetry with well-known journals and presses; former slammers Patricia Smith and Tyehimba Jess, for example, both recently wrote books selected for the National Poetry Series. Still others go on to teach literature or performance at colleges and public schools; slam poetry veterans now teach at institutions such as Sarah Lawrence College, the University of Chicago, and the University of Southern California, Long Beach. For poets such as Tracie Morris, Derrick Brown, C. R. Avery, or Cin Salach, the slam has led them to avant-garde experiments in poetry and sound, while the slam itself remains popular and populist. This cross section of artists proves that, although one may compete in the slam only briefly, the influence of its marriage of verse and performance is wide and profound. It also proves that, although the slam may be limited by certain rules of competition, its fusion of genres inspires work that goes far beyond those boundaries and in many directions.

What has been missing from the criticism of slam poetry is its consideration on its own terms. Literary scholars have considered slam poetry haphazardly from perspectives of textual craft and orality. Some performance scholars and theater reviewers have tried to chronicle commonalities of slam delivery or have taken an ethnographic approach to describing a handful of poets' performance styles. But no one has yet considered slam poetry from the full range of disciplines and traditions it engages, and its criticism has been the poorer for it. Slam poetry is performed poetry, but it is also much more than conventional text put into performance. Its native venue is live performance, but it also is created and appreciated in print, through audio recordings, on video, and in broadcasts. What has perhaps been missing most markedly from criticism of slam poetry is serious consideration of the issues of identity and cultural politics that infuse its every aspect from the page to the stage, from composition to performance. My approach to the topic of slam poetry is to consider it as its own genre of work that combines literary, theatrical, political, and cultural influences and traditions. Only by contemplating it from these many perspectives will one get a clear idea of why artists and audiences find the slam so compelling—and also why, even after years of success and creative production, the vast majority of poets involved with the slam end up leaving the competition for other pursuits.

With these perspectives in mind, I outline slam poetry in chapter 1 as its own hybrid genre of verse, one that negotiates the possibilities and problems of text, performance, orality, and politics. Slam poetry is verse that exists most richly in a live dynamic between authors and audiences, and it displays the qualities of popular entertainment, adaptability across media and performance contexts, competitive argumentation, and self-conscious performances of the author's identity alongside narratives of marginalization. The topic of authenticity of the author's identity, especially racial identity, has been a theme in other performance poetry-cum-social movements including the Beat and Black Arts movements and even dating back to antebellum blackface performances enacting verse through recitation and song. In chapter 2, I consider these movements as precursors to the slam poetry movement, and taken together they suggest a link between authenticity and performances of blackness lying at the heart of American popular culture. Recognizing that identity is both performed and performative, I look to poetry slams in chapter 3 as sites where poets claim, negotiate, and sometimes refigure marginalized identities through performance. Many slam poets performing narratives about marginalized identities do little beyond expressing a sense of oppression, thereby reifying their positions as marginal, but some poets use parody and persona to inventively flip the script of marginality itself, and these performances signal the social and political possibilities of slam performance. In chapter 4, I consider the impact of slam poetry's commercial foil, spoken word poetry, and its associations with hip-hop music and performances of urban underclass blackness through mainstream media projects such as the film *Slam* and *Russell Simmons Presents Def Poetry.* Participating in these projects allows African American artists an opportunity to reach larger mainstream audiences while simultaneously making them a spectacle for consumption by predominantly white, middle class audiences—a position that has obvious pros and cons.

As one of the first scholarly works to explore the politics of identity in slam poetry, a genre that is itself just gaining scholarly attention, this book aims to be suggestive, not definitive. It will take time to determine whether slam poetry will render Whitman's great audience as it will take time for scholars to situate it in literary and theatrical traditions. It is quite possible that, like Beat and Black Arts poetry, slam poetry will be defined by the cultural-historical moment in which it was produced—destined to fail outside of its moment but also influencing work beyond its current purview to push American poetry in new directions. It is also quite possible that, like these movements, slam poetry will be subsumed into the academy, the institution to which it was first built in opposition. Even as poets continue to characterize a classic tension between the academy and popular culture, slam poetry might be, in the end, about building bridges, not walls, between these two audiences for poetry. This book is one step in that direction.

CHAPTER ONE

On Page and Stage

Slam Poetry as a Genre

In trying to isolate its appeal to contemporary audiences, scholars have mainly focused on the orality of slam poetry—on the transmission of an original poetic text through speaking. For example, in his 2004 essay "Disappearing Ink," Dana Gioia characterizes the reemergence of popular poetry through rap, cowboy poetry, and poetry slams as an oral phenomenon. The relationship between audiences and popular poetry, he argues, is largely mediated by methods other than print, recalling poetry's preliterate origins and reflecting an "oral culture" now changing the landscape of the literary arts.[1] In this, Gioia echoes a number of other scholars who have focused on poetry's orality, including Charles Bernstein, Walter Ong, and Paul Zumthor. Other scholars, such as Gregory Nagy, have traced slam back to ancient oral traditions—those of griots, the bards, or the Homeric epic.[2] Although the importance of contemporary poetry's life in media other than print should not be underestimated, a sole scholarly focus on the oral and aural—on speaking and listening—is, I believe, a little misguided. Even though such analyses are critically sound, they miss the mark in exploring what poets and audiences find truly compelling about slam poetry: the larger cultural and political dynamics it enacts through performance.

Orality itself is neither the ultimate characteristic of verse's current popularity nor its most crucial. Especially in the case of slam poetry, orality is but one component in a poem's presentation. It is the range of performative aspects of a poem—vocal dynamics, physical dynamics, appearance, setting, hoots and hollers from the audience itself—that influences one's experience of a slam poem. Slams are theatrical events, not listening booths, and what proves compelling to audiences is that such events performatively embody verse and its author. With this in mind, it becomes clear that the popular appeal of slam poetry relies on, and indeed creates, not just an oral culture but a performative culture.

The distinction between the oral and the performative is an important one to make as it marks the difference between poetry's transmission and reception. Slam poetry's following has been gained not merely through the act of listening; although CDs and MP3s are a popular way of documenting slam poetry, such verse is created to be best understood in live performance. In live venues (as well as audiovisual media), appreciating poetry becomes a multisensory experience. Audiences don't merely listen to a poem; they react to an entire performance of verse, at times performing right back through applause, spiteful hissing, or comments shouted to the poet or slam host. Audiences receive performed verse by experiencing how the poet moves, appears, sounds, and physically embodies the poem. The Pulitzer-prize-winning poet Henry Taylor notes that those regularly attending poetry performances "are there for something other than the purity of oral performance" and are instead looking for physical or vocal habits of the author that "might deepen the feeling of personal encounter with the poetry."[3] What makes slam poetry popular is that it brings verse to be performed in certain ways: expressed with and through particular dialects, formats, gestures, and renegade attitudes that underscore its sense of urgency and authenticity.

The current critical emphasis on orality also ignores the importance of the role of the author in slam poetry. Far from harkening back to poetry's preliterate origins in which the boundaries of authorship were muddied by oral transmission, slam poetry puts exceptional emphasis on the role of the author and his or her identity. In fact, the rules governing national slam competition stipulate that the performer of a slam poem must also always be its author. In slam performances, just as in poetry readings where poems are read aloud by their authors, one can witness larger ideas about authorship, identity, and audience at work in poetry's physical and vocal performance. In this way, poetry slams and readings are similar, although they often differ in tone, energy, and audience expectation—qualities fueled, no doubt, by the slam's competitive structure.

Slam poetry does not exist in reference to a preliterate origin, nor is it extraliterate, as critics focusing on orality may suggest. Such an emphasis serves to erase slam poetry's relationship with text, which, though diminished, is still very much present. Slam poets may appear to improvise or spontaneously recite their work, but in actuality most of their performances are the product of painstaking hours of composition, memorization, choreography, and rehearsal. Although a handful of slam poets freestyle, the vast majority memorize from written work, and some even choose to perform their poetry while reading from the page. The fact that almost all slam poems are executed in print and yet are intended for performance ensures a chimeric relationship with text. Slam poets sell CDs and DVDs of their work and may perform on television or in films; at the same time, they also peddle self-published chapbooks or full-length print collections. Such publications are indicative of their wish to move within and between several types of media, occupying poetry's traditional abode of print while also existing in the oral and performative contexts of audio recordings, television, film, and live performance. This sets slam poetry apart from performance scripts such as screenplays or theatrical plays, for although slam poetry is meant to best be appreciated in live performance, it can also strive to be appreciated in print alone and apart from the standards of performance.

That said, even as slam poetry moves within and between different media, the context of live performance shines a particularly bright light into its inner workings, especially as those workings involve performances of identity. In this context, all slam poems become about the author's performance of identity on some level because of the author's mandated presence onstage. His or her speech, dress, gestures, voice, body, and so on all reflect in some way on the poem at hand, and these various aspects of embodiment convey nuances of cultural difference that the page cannot. With the author's embodiment, members of the audience are instantly privy to the physical and performative markers of identity that consciously or unconsciously inform their understanding of the poem through certain cultural lenses. In this way, slam poetry engages a whole host of cultural and political complexities before an author even opens his or her mouth. It also suggests that poetry slams can be places where these complexities of identity can be better examined, and in this regard they are places of fascination and possibility.

All of this is to say that slam poetry lives on both the page and the stage, and it may meet varying degrees of success in either venue. As such, standards of composition and performance have arisen that separate slam from other types of performance poetry (such as poetry based in performance art or theatrical readings of verse) so that one can consider slam poetry its own genre of creative work. Some slammers balk at such a generic distinction, citing the fact that slams remain open to all comers and therefore there can be no such thing as slam poetry. Others embrace the classification, hoping to legitimize the genre or, conversely, to associate themselves with slam poetry's renegade status in the literary world. Regardless of which camp they are in, most poets involved with the slam will agree that, although not all poetry performed at slams can be considered slam poetry, many poets adhere to certain standards of writing and performance to achieve slam success. These standards have in many cases led to formulaic work—a political rant, for example, or a fierce declaration of one's identity—but in their fusion of poetry and performance, poets also innovate in both fields.

Many may define slam poetry merely by its seemingly narrow range of content, which includes confessional narratives, diatribes about popular culture, and sociopolitical critiques. Others would do so by noting its common modes of address, which range from loud confrontational delivery to over-the-top comedic bids for the audience's favor. Others might also try to recognize slam poetry by means of formal characteristics of language such as regular rhyme, repeating meter, or use of a refrain. These formal characteristics often reflect the influence of hip-hop; indeed, regularly rhymed poetry is usually recognized by poets and audience members as extensions of a hip-hop tradition not as formalist poetry.[4]

Still, poets perform work at slams that falls outside of these usual rubrics, making it difficult to isolate particular subjects, modes of address, or formal qualities that all slam poetry shares on a universal level. Instead, slam poetry is defined less by its formal characteristics and more by what it wishes to achieve or effect: a more immediate, personal, and authentic engagement with its audience. When reflecting on the effects of slam poetry's composition and performance, four main qualities emerge as most common. First, slam poetry aims to actively engage and entertain its audience, sometimes confrontationally, through live performance. In doing so, it exhibits adaptability in and across different contexts, venues, audiences, and media. Second, since it is judged in a competitive format, slam poetry makes an argument that attempts to influence (and sometimes instruct) its audience. In this respect, it often includes a demonstrative condemnation or elevation of a speaker or subject (what rhetoricians know as epideictic oratory). Third, since the rules of the National Poetry Slam dictate that poems must be performed by their authors, authorship itself becomes a self-conscious performance. Because the slam format demands that the "I" of the page must also be the "I" of the stage, slam poetry leads to a hyperawareness of the first-person speaker, manifested most commonly in the performance of the author's identity. This performance of self takes place even when the slam poet is not writing in the first person. Finally, slam poetry is largely dedicated to the ideals of democracy, equality, and diversity. These ideals surface through the practice of slams, and frequently as some aspect of the poetry itself, inviting (and at times demanding) a shared sense of liberalism and tolerance among those in attendance.

At the heart of each of these aspects of slam poetry is the complex exchange between slam poets and their audiences. Rather than engaging in the relatively passive dynamics of reading print or listening to a poetry reading, slam poetry, facilitated by performance, commands that the poet, poem, and audience have an immediate and active critical relationship with one another. Furthermore, it seals the author's intimate and inseparable role as the embodiment of poem's commonly first-person voice in performance. Slam poetry declares that its authors are alive and well, leaving little question in an audience's mind as to who is speaking. Such an association brings with it demands on slam poets, making them immediately accountable for the viewpoints expressed within their poems. Over the years, poems about identity and politics have proliferated on the slam stage, a trend that strongly underlines the role of authorship in slam poetry and makes overt the presentations of self (or selves) that have always been an aspect of slam performance.

Just as National Poetry Month, the Favorite Poem Project, and Poetry in Motion campaigns have tried to revise and strengthen the relationship between popular audiences and poetry, poetry slams offer a more inclusive vision of who can appreciate verse. The difference between slam and these projects lies in the dynamics of their criticism and judgments of poetic taste. In organized national projects, poets and poems are selected as worthy of attention by some critical body apart from their audience. Even in the case of the Favorite Poem Project, which is ostensibly open to anyone reading aloud the work of his or her favorite poet, editors select verses by largely canonical or established poets to be made public on the project's Web site, on DVDs, and in anthologies. Poetry slams, on the other hand, ask audiences to determine the worth of a poem through applause and scoring, eliminating the aesthetic filter of the editor altogether, in effect putting the audience in the dual seats of consumer and evaluator with no critical middleman. This results in an abundance of amateurish poetry at slams, but it also signals a more direct and open system through which audiences can appreciate and reward poetry of their own choosing.

The idea that the audience for poetry—not the poet or the critic—is the judge of literary taste is quite remarkable considering that a mere fifty years ago New Criticism called for poetry to be evaluated as a timeless artifact apart from the meddling presence of author or reader. Maria Damon remarks that poetry slams "offer an important venue for grassroots poetic activity that rewrites the privatistic lyric scene into a site for public discourse."[5] Experiencing poetry through slams becomes not about the private, author-to-audience act of reading print but about a public, dialogic communication between author and audience. Poetry slams embody real-time discursive critical acts. While some still argue that art should be independent of the popular tastes and demands of the day, slam poetry is often a staunch declaration of the now; in fact, it is not uncommon for a slam poem to be considered old hat a year or two after its first performance. This immediate, often urgent relationship between the slam poet and the audience is at the heart of understanding the appeal of such work, and in studying that relationship a more accurate portrait of slam poetry's contributions to performative culture can emerge.

Entertainment and Slam Poetry

One of the most noted aspects of slam poetry—and also one of the most reviled by its critics—is its entertainment quotient. Some academic critics have panned slams altogether for this quality. Harold Bloom, for example, remarked in an issue of the *Paris Review:*

> [O]f course, now it's all gone to hell. I can't bear these accounts I read in the *Times* and elsewhere of these poetry slams, in which various young men and women in various late-spots are declaiming rant and nonsense at each other. The whole thing is judged by an applause meter which is actually not there, but might as well be. This isn't even silly; it is the death of art.[6]

The political "rant" common to many poetry slams is not denied by slam practitioners; in fact, this aspect is celebrated by many slam poets and is often rewarded by audiences. However, slam poetry's accessibility and popularity should not be considered factors that automatically exclude quality. Instead, its accessibility and popularity are extensions of slam poetry's commitment to pleasing its audience. Bloom suggests in his statement that popularity and artistic merit are mutually exclusive, that what is deemed great by an invisible "applause meter" cannot be good poetry. Slam poets are quick to admit that a poem's high score does not ensure its poetic merit; a common conciliatory saying among competitors is "The best poem always loses." It is understood among poets that what slam audiences reward are things *in excess* of the poem itself, be it performance or politics or any other of the myriad factors that may cause an infatuation with a poet at a particular moment.

On the issue of poetic taste, and the always fraught and usually untenable argument that an entire mode of poetic expression is wholly "good" or "bad," consider the statement of journalist and publisher Luis Rodriguez.

> There is a pendulum swing when it comes to discussing performance in poetry: it's either the best thing to happen to poetry or the worst. The gist of most critiques of the concept of poetry performance seems to say that "good" poetry is linked to the academy, and thus to the page, while "bad" poetry is rooted in the inarticulate, illiterate masses (and often relegated to the stage).[7]

This seems to be the underlying tenet of Bloom's statement, one that his loyalty to a Great Authors curriculum further suggests. There are similarly polemic but ultimately reductive arguments that some practitioners of slam proclaim: that slam poetry is a utopian celebration of orality and diversity, producing a "revolutionary" community of writers and listeners while elitist academic poets further cement themselves in ivory towers clutching texts by dead white men. Despite the frequent use of this latter rhetoric (not only by today's slam poets but by poets ascribing to many other performance poetry movements) and some critics' use of the former, neither is an accurate portrait of what slam poetry is and does. In fact, this War of the Roses between academic and popular verse, as well as the discourse surrounding it, is more indicative of the cultural politics of contemporary poetry than single judgments of taste or quality ever could be.

Slam poetry aims to be consumable, not difficult or inaccessible, because, as the veteran slammer Jack McCarthy remarks, "Audiences do not award any points for degrees of difficulty. What we do is not a diving competition. It is a competition for the hearts and minds of a live audience, and the key to their hearts and minds is their attention."[8] The focus on gaining such attention has led many slam poets to emphasize the entertainment value of their writing and performance. In this respect, slam poetry best resembles show business; poets use what they think will be humorous, verbally impressive, or dramatic in order to compete with each other. It also has led to more than one slam poet shouting or speeding through a poem in an attempt to give it emphasis; it is the seasoned slam poet who knows that the quieter poem can gain the most attention in an otherwise noisy room.

In creating the slam rules and format, Marc Smith admits that he was initially looking for a place to gain praise for his poetry in front of a larger audience.[9] To do so, he relied on the passion and excitement induced by live entertainment.[10] Of course, this sense of entertainment can be achieved in a number of ways; the range of approaches used to capture an audience's attention is as varied as the slam performers themselves. New York poet Patricia Smith commands a room with a forceful and authoritative voice, Boston poet Jack McCarthy quietly employs confessional narrative to gain his following, Chicago poet Regie Gibson delivers his work with jazz-inspired rhythms and vocal tones, and Los Angeles poet Beau Sia delivers politically inspired punch lines about his Asian American identity at a frenetic pace. Comedy, parody, gravitas, outrage, sensuality—all may be used to engage and entertain slam audiences. Although it may seem strange for a three-minute political rant to be considered entertaining, audiences often reward confrontational or angry slam performances. Such conviction and passion are inevitably deemed authentic by many audiences, and it is often a more passionate and seemingly authentic connection to the subject and author of verse—not the artificial hushed and reverent tone of a traditional poetry reading—that they seek in coming to a slam. Veteran slammer Taylor Mali (who has a CD titled *Conviction*) partially attributes slam poetry's popularity to this aspect of its performance: "People love to see anyone who believes strongly in something, perhaps because so few people do these days."[11]

At slams, many of which occur in noisy and crowded bars or clubs, poets are encouraged to do what they can outside of the usual script of the poetry reading to encourage the audience to listen.[12] Some poets achieve this by performing off-mic, performing poems while moving through the audience (Marc Smith himself is famous for this technique, crawling atop tables and chairs if need be); by shouting or singing; or even by performing choreographed moves or acrobatics as part of the poem's performance (Austin slammer DaShade is known for a poem in which he performs flips and capoeira moves as part of his performance). Such tactics have yielded the criticism—sometimes from its own practitioners—that slam poetry "courts its audience too assiduously" and is "more entertainment than art."[13] McCarthy admits that in order to win an audience's attention slam poets "have to make some concessions" regarding the difficulty of the poetic craft.[14] Some poets have even fallen into a recognizable and somewhat hackneyed pattern of confrontation in order to please their audiences. John McWhorter of *Commentary* notes that "at places like the Nuyorican Café in New York, the poets who tend to move audiences the most are the ones channeling a formulaic rage."[15] Still there is no doubt that such tactics are also effective in yielding a greater popular audience for the slam. Composing and performing poetry to emphasize more "showy" elements may be done for the sake of audience approval, but slam poets also argue that their work serves this higher purpose.

Thus, although slam poetry, like much poetry in general, still puts a premium on the importance of the author (an issue I will discuss in a moment), the genre puts a similar premium on the service of its audience. In a spectacular role reversal of a traditional poetry reading, which usually asks its audience to be silently and passively receptive, poetry slams put the audience in the seat of critical power, asking them to immediately and overtly evaluate performed poetry through applause, shouting, and scoring. Some emcees of poetry slams—Marc Smith among them—even encourage audiences to shout approval or hiss disapproval *during* the performance of poetry. In this performative dialectic, poetry slams serve as soapboxes for audiences as well as poets. The slam audience's active role may appear vaudevillian; Amiri Baraka has argued that poetry slams "make the poetry a carnival—the equivalent of a strong-man act. They will do to the poetry movement what they did to rap: give it a quick shot in the butt and elevate it to commercial showiness, emphasizing the most backward elements."[16] Indeed, slam's emphasis on audience participation has led to poets being booed off the stage or receiving wild standing ovations. Still, no one can deny that audiences enjoy being vocal critics at these events, and the emphasis on audience engagement is one of the major reasons why slam poetry has gained such a following in the United States. "Turning a poetry reading into a 'show' was a revolutionary idea," says Marc Smith, "and it . . . is the reason the slam has flourished."[17] The New York poet and Bowery Poetry Club owner Bob Holman sums up the power of the slam audience this way.

> We are gathered here today
> because we are not gathered
> somewhere else today, and
> we don't know what we're doing
> so you do—the Purpose of SLAM!
> being to fill your hungry ears . . .
>
> . . . .
> We refuse
> to meld the contradictions but
> will always walk the razor
> for your love.[18]

The fact that slam poets, as Holman suggests, look to their audiences for purposefulness and praise is indicative of the importance live performance has in the slam poetry movement. Although live performance is not a hard-and-fast definitional contingent of the slam poem (since slam poems also exist in print, audio, and video media), live performance is often important to its composition. Many slam poems are composed with performative elements in mind that are meant to arouse a response from a live audience, and they may be written in language that is easy to comprehend on only one hearing. Devices such as repetition and rhyme, which may seem redundant on the page, similarly help guide the live audience through the poem in performance.

Slam poetry also exhibits a certain fluidity and adaptability in writing and performance. In addition to selecting poems they feel will be best received by a given audience, slam poets adapt the language, tone, speed, and energy of a poem to different contexts, audiences, and venues. For example, a poet is likely to make different choices when performing in front of regulars at a sports bar than when in front of students in a large high school auditorium, and these choices involve both the performance of the poem and its language. In composing their poetry, some slam poets perform drafts of their writing at slams, gauge audience reaction to those drafts, and then edit their poetry to make it more competitive or popular. Occasionally, competing poets will make on-the-spot changes to poems in order to riff off of (and thereby competitively capitalize on) work performed earlier in the slam, or, like lead singers in touring rock bands, they will add specific details about the venue or host city in their writing. Finally, the experienced slam poet usually has a range of work—funny, personal, serious, political—at his or her disposal in order to hit the right note with an audience at the right time.

As a result of this adaptability, an exclusive original of a slam poem does not exist in either print or performance. Instead, slam poems have multiple "original moments" as they are performed over and over again and change both in performance and content to suit different live audiences. Audio, video, and digital recordings of slam poetry—all of which lie at the nexus of liveness, mediation, and commodity—similarly trouble the notion of a single original moment ("Is it live or is it Memorex?"). The slipperiness of the slam poem is that it exists both everywhere and nowhere at once: it may exist as text or in performance bounded by space and time or as utterance and image in recorded media. The audience determines where the poem lives at any given moment, and this highly interactive relationship between author and audience is what sets slam poetry apart from both textual poetry and most other branches of performance poetry.[19]

Competition and Slam Poetry

Another aspect that sets slam poetry apart from other movements in contemporary poetry is its presentation within a competitive format. Not only are slam poets competing for an audience's attention, but they are also competing for the cold, hard math of scores that will determine their ranking among their competitors. In this respect, poetry slams can resemble forensics meets, with all participants trying to persuade an audience to agree that their poetry is the best performed at the event. This often manifests itself in the fierce expression of an argument or opinion; more specifically, slam poems often culminate in political arguments condemning racist or sexist attitudes or provide observational humor about contemporary culture or identity. As such, slam poems can take the form of epideictic oratory—the condemnation or praise of a speaker or subject. "Take Them Back," by the late Boston poet Lisa

King, is such a condemnation of the U.S. government's lack of response to the AIDS crisis during the Reagan era.

the truth about AIDS is
if jesus were here today his blood would be tainted
and you would call him
unclean
jerry falwell
you would call him
enemy
pat robertson
you would both try to raise money
to buy the nails[20]

Such passion and conviction in slam poetry has many sources, not the least of which is the slam poet's unflagging dedication to political beliefs. Another root of this conviction is slam poetry's competitive aspect. In order to be successful with their audiences, slam poets must convey a confidence in their writing and subject matter. In competing with each other, some slam poets may emphasize or even exaggerate this sense of confidence, resulting in over-the-top, didactic displays of comedy or political critique (and sometimes both). They may also overtly boast about their lyrical skills compared to their competitors' skills. This contest of conviction is a major component of the tone that many poetry slams take—and it seems that the higher the stakes of competition the more intense this sense of conviction becomes. At the National Poetry Slam, a few poets have been known to tip the mic stand over at the end of a poem or throw the microphone down on the stage in a final gesture of conviction—a faux pas in many performance circles. Such was the case at the 2002 NPS, where individual competitor Rives concluded one of his poems with the sentence "I told myself, 'If you get there, don't just rock the mic, tip the bitch over,'" after which he did just that.[21]

What slam poets compete for—at least most immediately—are scores given by judges from the audience. In national team competition, scores are decided in "bouts" where teams of poets are pitted against each other tournament style via a random draw. Poems performed at the bout are scored by five members of the audience, and scores range from 0.0 to 10.0 using increments of a tenth of a point.

These judges are selected by the slam host or event staff from volunteers in the audience. Usually a good attempt is made to vary these judges in terms of race, gender, and age to avoid any appearance of discriminatory bias, although this variety is sometimes limited by audience demographics and audience members' willingness to judge. After competitors draw numbers out of a hat to determine the order of their performances, the judges assign a scores after each performance of a poem. Judges are not afforded anonymity; after each poem, the scores are announced onstage by the host. A scorekeeper drops the highest and lowest of these five scores, and the remaining three are added together to result in the poet's score for the round (for a maximum of thirty points). Each poem is also carefully timed by an official timekeeper; if the poets go over the allotted three minutes and ten seconds allowed by the NPS rules, they incur a half-point deduction from their score for every ten seconds in excess of the time limit. After three or four rounds of competition, the scores from each round are added to create a cumulative score for a team, and the team with the highest cumulative score wins the bout.[22]

Because poetry slams have flourished nationally and internationally under a competitive structure, standardized rules of competition have emerged and a nonprofit organization, Poetry Slam, Incorporated (formerly headed by Marc Smith, who holds the honorary title "president for life"), has been established to administer them. Every spring, a meeting is held to debate and vote on PSI rules, tournament structure, and slam community issues. This meeting is attended by "slammasters," persons appointed or elected to the national organization to represent the interests of certified local slam venues.

The high-stakes atmosphere of the National Poetry Slam competitions has led slam poets to strategize how and when to perform their poetry at the slam so as to maximize their scores. *Score creep,* a term poets use to describe overall higher scores in later rounds relative to earlier ones (and, on occasion, to describe an overly competitive poet), is a codified phenomenon at slams. Slam poets have a host of strategies to combat or capitalize on score creep. Most slams also offer a "calibration poet" (colloquially known as a "sacrificial poet" or "sacrificial goat"), who performs before the first round of competition in order to allow judges to practice scoring. Still, scores are inevitably lower in the first few performance slots, and going first—or even early—in the competition can be a significant handicap. Strategies to win slams range from simple—such as following a mediocre piece of comedy with a howler so as to demonstrate superiority over one's competitors—to complex—such as establishing "natural sets" and "resonance" between certain poems based on performance order.[23] Taylor Mali, whose notoriety in the slam community stems from his zeal for strategy and his presence on an unprecedented four championship teams, went so far to publish a chapbook of slam strategies, which includes tactics as intricate as "Working the Flashpoint Position" and as crass as "Don't Lead with Your Lesbian."[24]

Such calculated angles to winning seem to fly in the face of the oft-quoted slammaster Allan Wolf, who states, "The points are not the point, the point is poetry."[25] Indeed, although slam poets cite an abiding loyalty to both poetry and poetry's community, the competitive aspect of slam poetry is a major source of its attractiveness to poets and audiences. "If the points were truly 'not the point,'" remarks the Seattle slam poet Jeremy Richards, "then they wouldn't lead to anything, wouldn't determine who gets the money, who makes it on the team, who gets on a plane and flies to Nationals to plaudits and opportunities reserved for the new slam elite."[26] As Richards suggests, the intensely competitive atmosphere of most National Poetry Slams is a clue that there is much more at stake than scores. Team titles have been worth cash prizes of up to two thousand dollars in the past. The Individual World Poetry Slam, also sponsored by PSI, began in 2004. In 2007, it featured seventy-two poets competing in one-, two-, three-, and four-minute rounds for a grand prize of twelve hundred dollars.[27] In addition to these prizes, a number of media opportunities that capitalize on the popularity of spoken word poetry have opened up for slam poets, including appearances on Russell Simmons's *Def Poetry* projects, film and theater engagements, commercial writing and voice-over work, and the opportunity to cut albums. Finally, poets compete to enhance their reputations as writers and performers. Even on a local level, slam poets compete for the esteem of their fellow poets and the larger literary community. Thus, slams are competitive events in that they can be career- and reputation-building opportunities.

Poets' bids for high scores, combined with slam poetry's greater media presence and popularity, have led to claims that slam poetry is growing more homogeneous in its themes and styles. Marc Smith laments:

As any good father does, I worry about the slam. Its growing success seems to threaten the eccentric nature of the art. More and more young poets copy the chops of someone they heard on a CD or saw on TV. They don't draw from their own experiences. They don't trust their own voices. I regret that the astounding variety of styles, characters, and subject matter present in the early years has, to some degree, been homogenized into a rhetorical style designed to score a "perfect 10." I also regret that many slam poets care more about building a career than they do about developing shows that offer communities, large and small, a much-needed poetic outlet.[28]

Most slam poets acknowledge this homogeneity in rhetorical style—the "formulaic rage" of loud, self-righteous declarations—while at the same time fiercely disavowing such homogeneity in their own work. Slam poets also, after hearing the same invectives over time, realize that the writing and performance they once thought of as refreshingly real is artificial and perhaps even derivative. This realization has led some slam poets to write invectives against slam poetry itself. When the veneer of authenticity and originality is stripped from the slam poem, what is left? This is the topic of the New York City poet Staceyann Chin, who performed her poem "I Don't Want to Slam" onstage at the final round of NPS competition in 2000.

> I don't want
> to join the staged revolution
> don't want to be part of just
> some spotlight-slamming solution
> don't want to go to Austin or Chicago[29]
> simply because I think I have
> the rapidly moving metaphors
> smashing off the Nuyorican walls
> or similes like a silver bullet
> bee-lining for the finals on a balloon
> full of nothing but hot air
> making the room smell like a fart
> from a bad poem that somebody
> should have said excuse me for

I don't want to just slam anymore
I don't want to sit
in smoke-filled rooms
listening to women who rhyme
creating lyrics that rock
making sure they fit within
the confines of some judge's ticking clock
smiling with people I've only seen
on the corner of an old SlamNation flyer
trying to get them to tell me
how to record that first CD
how to really work a crowd
how to fuck those hard to please judges
so I can give birth to a bastard TEN

I'm tired of igniting blazes on the mike
pimping poems about my lover's private life
sipping iced teas over superlatives
eating spring rolls over hyperboles
juxtaposing myself in vegetarian cafes
between guys with funny sounding names
like Guy and Procope and Dot
hoping some of what makes them real poets
will rub off on a pretender like me[30]

In this excerpt, it is clear that while lamenting the homogeneous results of slam poetry's competitive aspect, Chin reveals many of the
rhetorical techniques common to slam style: staged calls for "revolution," frequent rhyme, use of "superlatives" and "hyperboles" to "work
a crowd," "pimping" confessional matter for scores, and an awareness
of the "ticking clock" and "hard to please judges." "I don't want to be /
a poet who just writes / for the slam anymore," she announces at the
opening of the poem. Instead she prefers the work of "real poets" such
as her named teammates and friends, and she engages in a moment of
self-critique, drawing a fine line between "real poets" and "poets who
write for the slam."

The irony here is, of course, that Chin uses some of the very same
techniques in her own writing—hyperbole, simile, rapidly moving
metaphor, invective—to critique the use of those techniques at poetry

slams, and in attempting to graduate from "pretender" to "poet" she must air this critique within the very competitive environment her poem declaims—the National Poetry Slam finals stage. As Chin demonstrates, being critically aware of the rhetorical chestnuts of slam poetry does not make one free of them. There are other aspects of the poem that indicate she wishes to harness slam poetry's power while disavowing the imperative to win. When it is performed in its entirety, Chin's poem runs well beyond the NPS time limit of three minutes ten seconds, and in a contest in which a tenth of a point commonly separates winners and losers, this ensures that the poem will not be competitive. Slam poets and most audience members recognize this as Chin's defiant gesture against the competitive structure of the poetry slam.

Performances of Authorship and Identity in Slam Poetry

Former U.S. poet laureate Billy Collins remarks that the public poetry reading "may convey the dramatic illusion that the words are issuing directly from the source," transforming authorship itself into a performance.[31] This is doubly true within the genre of slam poetry because of the crucially visible role of the author in slam writing and performance. The rules of the National Poetry Slam require a poet to "perform work that s/he has created" or, in the case of a group performance put in a single performer's competitive slot, to have contributed enough to the poem to be considered a "primary author" of it (see appendix, document 1).[32] In fact, controversy arose in 1996 when it was suspected that a team competing at NPS had used both a group piece written entirely by one team member and another poem written and performed exclusively by the same team member; therefore, not all members of the team were represented in terms of authorship over the course of the bout. As the NPS grows and the tournament structure changes to accommodate more teams and team members, rules about primary authorship continue to be a hot topic of debate.

Because NPS rules ensure that at slams authors are also always performers and vice versa, audiences commonly conflate the voice of the poem with that of the author. Through the sheer format of the competition, audiences are encouraged to see slam performances as confessional moments in which the "I" of the poem is also the "I" of the author-performer. Further encouraging this conflation is the common mode of address in slam poetry. Although work written in the second and third person does surface at poetry slams, the mode of address overwhelmingly chosen by slam poets is the first person. In Gary Mex Glazner's anthology *Poetry Slam,* for example, eighty-five out of one hundred poems are written in this voice.

This conflation is further underscored by a compositional emphasis on declarations of the self in slam poetry. Because the slam format encourages the "I" of the page to also be the "I" of the stage, there is a hyperawareness of self among slam poets and audiences, one that manifests itself most commonly through the author's performance of identity. One of the undisputed masters of this type of declaration is Saul Williams, who weaves statements of self-definition with hip-hop sensibilities and a cosmic spiritual awareness, as in his poem "Amethyst Rocks."

> I'll be in sync with the moon
> while you run from the sun
> life of the womb
> reflected by guns
> worshipper of moons
> i am the sun
> and I am public enemy number one
> one one one
> one one one
> that's seven
> and I'll be out on the block
>
> hustlin' culture
> slingin' amethyst rocks[33]

"Amethyst Rocks" is a critique of street hustlers and criminal life, which instead favors Williams's position as a poet, a self-proclaimed "hustler of culture." Poems such as this exemplify the hyperawareness of the author in slam poetry through the urge to define and proclaim one's self in both writing and performance.

Not all slam poems addressing identity take themselves so seriously, however. Genevieve Van Cleve's "I Was the Worst Feminist in the World" explores political identity through comedy. With acid quips about how she never quite fit the stereotype that her fellow women's studies students reflected—"Gloria Steinem and *The Feminine Mystique* were that much exhaust out of the back of a Volkswagen bus, late for a Jerry Garcia Memorial Service"—Van Cleve sends up the fruitless artificialities of her college feminist career while still affirming her commitment to and belief in feminism.

> I felt like freakish Mr. Rourke—Ricardo Monta-blonde in a rich,
> Corinthian leather miniskirt—the ringmaster of a Vaginal
>   Fantasy Island—
> Registering voters—Smiles everyone—
> Protecting clinics—Smiles everyone—
> Marching in interlocking circles in the name of vaginal pride—
> Smiles, everyone . . .

> Marching in interlocking circles which led us back to each other,
>   biting and scratching, sipping our saucers of milk, comparing
>   our relative levels of victimization. And as we were wringing
>   our hands, they were kicking our asses—need I remind you of
>   Professor Anita Hill, Lani Guinier, or the slaughters in the
>   clinics of Boston? We have not stopped them from blaming
>   single mothers, lesbians, and every other slit with a vision, a
>   voice, or a problem in this country. Need I remind you?

> But forgive my pedanticism. Forgive my ire. I do have a
>   tendency to run my mouth.

> I am usually a goddamn ray of sunshine.[34]

When these last lines are performed in Van Cleve's thick, hospitable Texan accent, the humor and the irony of the poem are clear. Van Cleve's negotiation of feminist identity on the slam stage illustrates that one's performance of self is capable of eliciting laughter as well as thoughtful or dramatic consideration. It also shows that a slam poem's political "pedanticism," as she puts it, can have a sense of humor.

In its emphasis on the author's proclamation of self, what slam poetry offers is the antithesis of philosopher Roland Barthes's "death of the author"—the idea that the text and its author are unrelated.[35] Slams and the poetry produced in and for them proclaim that the author is alive and well. They insist that the author not only be present but is an inherent and necessary part of the performed poem. In its emphasis on the first person in composition—on the performance of self and identity—and with the requirement that authors must perform their own work, the genre goes beyond mere confessionalism. Slam poetry entails not only an admission of authorial self but an outright proclamation of authorial self through performance. In this way, the identity of the author is inextricably linked to the slam poem, both in writing and performance, because the author is proclaiming an aspect of self in the poem and performing that self onstage.

Even when a slam poem does not take identity as its subject matter, the slam poet is always, in performing the poem's voice, enacting aspects of identity onstage. Take, for example, Tara Betts's "Rock 'n' Roll Be a Black Woman." Even though the poem is not written in the first person, Betts very much performs characteristics associated with African American blues women, as in this excerpt.

Rock 'n' Roll be a Black Woman
Where you thank they got the name from?
Black Magic Woman
Brown Sugar
Copper strings stretched out on guitar necks
Tan skirts taut on the mouth of drums

Rock 'n' Roll be a Black Woman
Plucking as firmly as
Mashing of frets like delicate testicles
jangling under the discord of a well-pedicured foot

Rock 'n' Roll be a Black Woman
Eminent as comet tail juice announcing
An ebony-tinged star's exit

Rock 'n' Roll be a Black Woman
Furiously embossing the stamp of her
man's ass into the mattress
Primacy screaming in the breasts that fed you
As tired sweat wriggled between them
She be tainted with funk
Permeatin her like chittlin buckets
in kitchen sinks[36]

In her writing, Betts exemplifies many tropes of African American blues women's performance: slinging vernacular ("thank," "Permeatin her like chittlin buckets," "funk"), harnessing the cleverness of figurative language ("like delicate testicles / jangling under the discord of a well-pedicured foot"), boasting of sexual power and stamina ("furiously embossing the stamp of her man's ass / into the mattress"), and reflecting perseverance through difficulty ("breasts that fed you / As tired sweat wriggled between them").[37] Betts also gives a formal nod to the blues, repeating "Rock 'n' Roll Be a Black Woman" as if it were a blues refrain. In her performance of this poem, Betts slightly exaggerates the cadence of the poem's vernacular, drawing out vowels and playing with its musicality. The normally soft-spoken Betts also physically embodies the strength of African American blues women, changing her posture to tower over her audience and projecting her voice to reach the back row. Thus, even though this is neither a persona poem nor written in the first person, Betts embodies in voice and physical stature the very "Black Magic Woman" of which she speaks.

This case is further illuminated by the implicit complexities of racial identity in Betts's performance, because Betts, a light-skinned woman who identifies as an African American with a mixed-race heritage, is not always hailed as black. Several of her poems deal explicitly with the perceived ambiguity of her racial identity (or identities), and although "Rock 'n' Roll Be a Black Woman" doesn't take up the author's racial hailing as an explicit topic of discussion, Betts's performance has the potential to do so. In embodying the formal and musical hallmarks of black blues women, Betts performs racial identity in a way that suggests her self-identification as African American even as her racial hailing—at least as it deals with aspects of physical appearance—may be ambiguous in other contexts. In this way, as it is performed through and in reference to the author's body, "Rock 'n' Roll Be a Black Woman" makes an audience's implicit assumptions about physical appearance and race explicit, providing a unique window of opportunity for the author and audience to explore them.

Slam poetry's unique emphasis on the issues of authorship and identity culminates, finally, around the issue of authenticity. As Bob Holman notes of slam's beginnings: "[O]nce the connection between spoken word / hip hop / performance / slam / political verse had begun, it completely swept away all other poetic forces. . . . There was a hunger to hear the single voice of the poet, speaking from the heart."[38] Audiences, on the whole, expect slam poets to deliver a more authentic brand of expression than traditional verse, one that promises a special sense of connection, conviction, or personal power. This has resulted in a particular emphasis on "truth" and "realness" within the genre of slam poetry, and it is this final—though most elusive—aspect of slam poetry's definition that informs the rest of this book.

Some slam poets have achieved this sense of closeness, as I have shown, by writing about and performing issues of identity, and a great many more make a claim to authenticity by engaging the politics of difference and social change. Such is the case with the end of Staceyann Chin's poem, "I Don't Want to Slam," which, while disavowing the slam's competitive framework, ends by arguing for the realness of her poetry because she believes it is a means of transformation.

> Today I want to write
> from a place where I change lives
> and change people and places
> cross over boundaries
> of sexes and cultures and races
> paint the skies deep red
> instead of boring blue
> write the true histories of me and you
>
> . . . .
>
> I want to write
> I left my lover and
> now I want her back poems
> I miss Jamaica
> but I'm never going back poems
> I know it's not a ten
> but it sends shivers down MY back poems
> poems that talk about life
> and love and laughter
> poems that reveal the flaws
> that make strikingly real people
> real poems
> poems that are so honest
> they slam[39]

Chin outlines a sense of "real" poetic practice here to produce a politically and socially informed sense of verse that reflects her identity as a lesbian and a Jamaican national. Ironically, even though she tries to place this type of practice outside of the arena of slam, Chin is actually repeating what most slam poets claim to do—using personal reflections to relate a certain sense of authenticity. Indeed, bids for authenticity—both implicit and explicit—may be the most defining aspect of the genre of slam poetry.

The final judge of this authenticity, however, is the slam audience. How do audiences weigh the truth of one person's expression or experience over another's? This is one of the motivating pursuits of this book, and such a question forces one to consider not just the literary and performance traditions embodied at poetry slams but the political and cultural dynamics at play between slam poets and their audiences. Discussing those lenses through which audience members receive and evaluate performances of the slam poet's identity can, in turn, tell us much about the "authentic" as a performative phenomenon in American popular culture at large.

With its populist strains for democracy and representations of "the people," slam resembles several other performance poetry movements, including the beat and black arts movements, and it even recalls earlier poetic and theatrical traditions of the antebellum period. Does an emphasis on authenticity and identity also surface in these other movements, and, if so, how can these movements inform our understanding of slam poetry? How do the populist and democratic strains of these movements influence who practices this verse and what audiences they reach? And, finally, how does race identity inform the performance and reception of such poetry?

CHAPTER TWO

Poetry and the People

The Cultural Tensions of American Popular Verse in Performance

If there's one lesson the academy might learn from the
slam, it's that the audience matters. Every poet, regardless
of how abstract or esoteric, should have at least one poem
he or she can read to a group of strangers on the subway.
    —Jeffrey McDaniel, "Slam and the Academy"

In America, the use of the term *popular verse* has a varied history. It has
been used to describe the lyric formality of rap, the nomadic and hip
strain of the Beats, the militant vernacular assumed by Black Arts poets, the populist practice of poetry slams, and even the jingles of radio
stations and television commercials. When literary critics speak of
American popular verse, they imply a poetry that exists outside of what
the poet Charles Bernstein has called "official verse culture," the cadre
of literary journals, conferences, and academic MFA programs that are
a mainstay of contemporary American poetry. It may be steeped in the
local, the vernacular, and the discourse of the marginal, insistent on accessibility while existing outside or on the boundaries of both dominant and academic culture. Popular verse is commonly infused with a
sense of historically defined "lowbrowness" which, it is assumed, popular audiences can recognize, identify with, and appreciate.

Slam poetry, as Jeffrey McDaniel suggests, is one such example of
popular verse. The tensions waged between American popular poetry
and both academic and dominant culture have quite a history, particularly as they happen to surface in performance. Such is the case with
the Beat movement, the Black Arts movement, and even the antebellum
tradition of blackface minstrelsy. The last of these has traditionally
been considered in a theatrical setting, but I wish to consider it as an
early stage for popular verse performance. Although each of these
movements in popular verse emerged from unique historical contexts,
they all circulated in conscious contrast to the academic verse and
dominant culture of their times, perpetuating particular ideas about
race, class, and nation in order to reach popular audiences.

As the variety of these movements may suggest, popular verse in performance is not bound to a particular style but is instead poetry that performs an attitude of resistance to a dominant literary elite, in today's terms the culture of MFA programs, the canon, and literary criticism. In this sense, popular verse is marginal, that is, it exists outside the dominant center of poetry's production, criticism, and reception, which is often located within academic culture. Popular verse in performance also engages in a larger tension with dominant culture, one often located in or embodied by the American white middle class. Its artists are bohemian, vagabond, militant, or otherwise countercultural. In many respects, popular verse's dual tensions with dominant and academic culture are inseparable, for popular poets often portray them as one and the same. Put in reductive but utterly familiar terms, both cultures are seen as realms of that vague and ominous oppressor, "the man."

Popular verse's quality of institutional and cultural resistance is more important than the size of its audience, although many popular poets have reached mass audiences through performance media such as film, video, television, and the Internet. Some have criticized popular performance poetry movements for only reaching a relatively small number of people in local readings; popular verse practitioners often make a similar allegation that academic poetry only reaches an elite group. Neither criticism is wholly accurate, although they both serve to feed popular poetry's dual tensions. Although it may also perform the same tensions, avant-garde performance poetry usually falls outside the purview of popular verse. Since such poetry aims to be ahead of contemporary taste, it often requires a certain knowledge or aesthetics to be accessible to popular audiences (and hence, to borrow McDaniel's rule of thumb, it may not be the best choice to read to a group of strangers on a subway).[1]

In his book *Poetry and the Public,* Joseph Harrington notes that in any given era American poetry is defined by its relationship with the public: as a way to take "refuge from the public," as a method of "engaging with the public," or as a way to negotiate public and private domains.[2] With this in mind, the contemporary tension between poetry in the private academy and the public realm of the popular signals a larger definitional debate about what poetry is and does, and by studying this tension one may better understand popular poetry's significance in the present moment. The tension between popular and academic verse is not necessarily an antagonistic force, even though it is often characterized as such. Rather, this discourse of tension serves to differentiate popular verse from its academic counterparts—so much so that it can invoke, specterlike, the very canon from which it stands in relief. Indeed, one cannot fully comprehend the popular appeal of slam poetry without having some sense of the literary judgments and expectations of academic culture. Ron Silliman calls this specter manifest at a poetry slam "ventriloquism of the canon," which "inhabit[s] the process of scoring, differentiating winners from losers . . . even when the judges are consciously 'antiacademic.'" Even at poetry readings, where literary critics are apparently absent, the ghost of their tastes and judgments linger in the minds of poets and audiences.[3] In such cases, academic and popular verse form a dialectic; one comes to influence the very definition and evaluation of the other. The theorist Stuart Hall remarks that this very same dialectic exists between popular and dominant culture; each is constituted in reference to the other.[4]

Keeping this in mind, it becomes clear that popular verse is not the voice of the people de facto. Instead, its poets' attitude of resistance and tension helps to construct and define the people's culture it claims to celebrate. In this constitutional capacity, popular poetry, its performance, and its discourses of tension can signify disruptions, discontinuities, and debates within American culture itself. Performances of popular poetry are not mere reflections of American popular culture. They are themselves sites of cultural contestation that help articulate and generate the very culture they claim to represent.

Still, in practice this discourse of tension looms so large that it is hard to perceive the popular-academic verse relationship as anything *but* antagonistic. Practitioners of popular verse may promote a strict or unnuanced sense of academic verse, and academic critics may similarly paint popular verse with broad, unflattering strokes. Caricature seems endemic to this discourse, as shown in a minstrel performer's sketch about going to college and learning about Lord Byron, who wrote "de book full ob poultry"; in Beat poet Allen Ginsberg's instructions to academics, "SQUARES SHUT UP and LEARN OR GO HOME"; or in canon defender Harold Bloom's dismissal of slam poetry as "rant and nonsense." It is not that such popular verse lies so extremely on one end of the cultural spectrum that it denies the lofty privileges of art. In fact, its poets often want to tout the glories of poetic tradition and may even claim canonical authors or traditions as inspirations. Still, popular poets wish to gain distance from both the academy and dominant culture, and many actively work to make this distinction clear through conscious choices in content, style, venue, or audience.

Exactly how certain American performance poetry movements that predate slam have achieved a sense of removal from academic verse and dominant culture is my topic here. Considering popular verse in performance with this single question in mind reveals not only a caricature of academic verse but also racial caricature, calls for nationalism, and specific appeals to working-class and antibourgeois audiences. My approach is intentionally selective, for although I could discuss many popular poetry movements and artists, Beat poetry, Black Arts Poetry, and the verse performance of blackface minstrelsy seem particularly relevant to understanding slam poets' performance of resistance to dominant culture and a literary elite. Since they occur in different cultural contexts and eras, these movements may seem disparate, and, indeed, their histories are far from linear. Still, when considered together they form a genealogy of popular poetry in performance in which common ideas of race, class, and nation are articulated to reach popular audiences and are recurring expressions of the tension between dominant and popular culture and academic and popular verse. Understanding the patterns of expression and reception in these movements can inform the way slam poetry engages similar tensions in a contemporary context, especially as it engages racial identity.

In order to contrast the real or perceived monolith of white male voices and standards of the academy and dominant culture, these movements have, on the whole and in ways appropriate to the era, taken up the shibboleth of blackness in order to access and represent "the people." For the Black Arts movement, representing African Americans and black aesthetic independence is a primary concern. For the Beat movement, African American culture and music provide a set of literary and performative aesthetics from which to draw. For blackface minstrelsy, counterfeit representations of blackness provide opportunities to parody and critique highbrow verse culture. For all of the movements I discuss, blackness serves as a complex and sometimes troubling emblem for the movement's marginality, for its distinction from dominant and academic cultures. Together they articulate a recurring race-class dynamic at the heart of U.S. popular culture enacted through the performance of popular verse.

Performance, Poetry, and Blackface Minstrelsy

The tradition of blackface performance—with its use of song, dance, the lyric, and rhyme—has much to offer in the way of understanding performance poetry's appeal to popular audiences. I begin with minstrelsy because of its explicit performances of blackness as implicit ways to reach popular audiences and because it has been hailed as "one of our [America's] first popular institutions."[5] It was also one of the first theatrical genres to cause a break between highbrow and lowbrow audiences. It is of interest because it was one of the first American forums where black "folk"—a term for "common" African Americans, but one that more specifically referred to rural southern blacks familiar with the plantation way of life—were represented onstage.[6] In truth, minstrelsy enacted an *idea* of blackness, one shaped by the relationships with and exchanges between African American folk and the whites portraying them onstage. Blackface performances included performances of plantation songs, dancing in the form of jigs and cakewalks, orchestral selections, monologues, and the occasional performance of popular verse, usually as part of a comedy routine or in song. Looking at blackface minstrelsy as a stage where popular verse is performed, often in contrast to academic poetry and highbrow culture, informs and enhances one's understanding of more contemporary performance poetry. Future poet-performers come to reflect, however inadvertently or remotely, the matrix of race, class, and national politics first engaged by blackface minstrelsy.

The American use of the term *minstrelsy* to describe this type of performance underlines blackface's literary ties since the term originated in European poetic and musical contexts. According to the *Oxford English Dictionary,* medieval minstrels entertained their audiences with stories, singing, dancing, buffoonery, and juggling. When used by Romantic poets, the term denoted a call to elevated, courtly lyricism—the performance or recitation of heroic or lyric poetry accompanied by music—a meaning that persists today. When minstrelsy was used to describe American blackface performances of the antebellum period, however, the term became associated with the buffoonery of black stereotypes such as the Uncle Tom, the plantation "darkey," or the northern dandy.[7] In this period, the etymology of minstrelsy bifurcated to connote two specific senses of the word: the implicitly white, highbrow minstrelsy of Europe's Romantics; and the black, lowbrow minstrelsy of what would soon become Jim Crow America. Thus, with the rise of blackface and its use of the term *minstrelsy* the image of the popular minstrel performer became both race and class specific. It also became particularly American as opposed to European.

Blackface minstrelsy has heretofore been considered a type of theater not a poetic expression. Yet when one considers the use of the lyric in minstrel performance (such as songs, lyrical sketches, and the recitation of parables or rhymes) the literary overtones of minstrel performance emerge to join its theatrical history. Keeping such acts in mind, antebellum blackface performance can be regarded as an early performance poetry movement in America, one that distinguished itself from other oral poetry movements across the globe through the use of blackness as a popular signifier and that helped establish a lyrical tradition born of American concerns about race, class, and nation.

Blackface performance began in the early nineteenth century and persisted through the early twentieth; blackface shows were known to be performed as late as the 1920s, although they were few and far between by that time. Individual performances of folk songs in blackface are reported to have taken place as early as 1799, but the minstrel tradition is generally acknowledged to have begun in 1843.[8] On February 6 of that year, the first blackface minstrel company, the Virginia Minstrels, performed at New York City's Bowery Amphitheatre. The four-person company—which included Billy Whitlock, Dick Pelham, Dan Emmett, and Frank Brower along with other rotating performers—set the standard for costuming and instrumental arrangement (the bones, tambourine, banjo, and squeeze box) of future minstrel companies.[9]

These performers also set the standard for a particular vision of blackness on the minstrel stage; they did not want to appear "too black" so that they were mistaken for actual "Negroes," but they still wished to appear black enough to be considered vessels of African American songs and performance traditions (see fig. 1). In fact, because early audiences often mistook minstrel performers for blacks,[10] it became common in the minstrel industry to feature images of performers in blackface next to images of them as "gentlemen" (i.e., without dark makeup and in formal dress) (see fig. 2). Some early companies even broke up their performances into programs in which company members performed patriotic or classic songs "as citizens" (whites) and popular selections "as Ethiopians," although the former of these acts was eventually dropped as blackface performance proved to be a more popular

*This is the first WOOD CUT ever made for a
Minstrel Company . It was so black that the
Virginia Minstrels sent it back...........1843*

*This is the print that was accepted
by the*
VIRGINIA MINSTRELS

FIG. 1. Virginia Minstrels woodcuts, 1843. Blackface performers were, from the start of the minstrel tradition, concerned with promoting a certain vision of blackness, one that wasn't "too black" and slightly belied the white performers under the burnt cork masks. The second image shows the standard costuming and basic instrumentation of a minstrel ensemble. (Scrapbook image courtesy of the Harry Ransom Humanities Research Center, The University of Texas at Austin.)

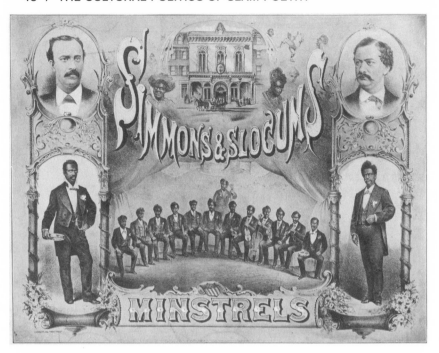

FIG. 2. Simmons & Slocums minstrel company promotional material, undated. Picturing key performers both in blackface and as "gentlemen" or "citizens" (i.e., as whites) was common in minstrel company advertisements, emphasizing the counterfeit and spectacular crossover from one racial category to another. (Image courtesy of the Harry Ransom Humanities Research Center, The University of Texas at Austin.)

attraction. This tension between what is "authentically" black and what is counterfeit resurfaces later in several performance poetry movements.

The division of early minstrel programs into performances as whites and "Negroes" (i.e., in blackface) also emphasized an important aspect of nationhood in antebellum America: citizenship. The Dred Scott case—which began in 1846 and lasted over a decade and through which the Supreme Court ultimately denied blacks citizenship—put the issue of black citizenship prominently in the public eye during the heyday of blackface performance.[11] Anxiety and curiosity about black citizenship was a theme that played out on the minstrel stage throughout the antebellum period. Even when programs were not divided into "citizen" and blackface programs, minstrel performances highlighted

disparities in citizenship through subject matter. Scenes from plantation life were staples of minstrel performances, and representations of
blackface performers as "Ethiopians" or plantation slaves explicitly
conjured the African American's alien status. Perhaps most important
to understanding the citizenship issue is the sheer act of citizen whites
wearing the burnt cork mask and consciously inhabiting the identity of
a noncitizen. Aside from the racial implications and complications inherent in that act, the alien status of African Americans was one of the
more important aspects that made taking on a black identity so liminal
in antebellum culture. This liminality was and is highly desirable as a
badge of resistance to dominant and academic cultures.

The racial dynamic engaged by minstrelsy—that of a mimetically
"black" performer entertaining predominately white audiences—car-
ries with it echoes of the master-slave relationship pivotal to regional
and national identity at that time. The scholar Simon Frith, in unpack-
ing the racial dynamics of twentieth-century rock and roll, suggests that
the legacy of black slaves performing for their masters' entertainment
"lies at the heart" of understanding the contemporary dynamic between black entertainers and white audiences, and, indeed, it under-
pins much of American popular entertainment and national culture.[12]
Even when such entertainment is racially counterfeited, as it is in
blackface minstrelsy, this dynamic still haunts its reception.

As one journalist of the period relates, blackface minstrel performers
came to be regarded, at least in a general sense, as poets of the people
who reflected and generated the lowbrow aesthetics and poetics of
blackness. The essayist James Kennard Jr. wrote in 1845 that "the Jim
Crows, the Zip Coons, and the Dandy Jims, who have electrified the
world, from them proceed our ONLY TRULY NATIONAL POETS."[13] As
a critic who disapproved of what he considered the baseness of minstrel performances, Kennard puts into sharp contrast the two race-
specific senses of the minstrel. That performances of blackness had not
only entered white culture but had come to define popular American
culture proved a source of anxiety for critics such as Kennard.

> Who are our true rulers? The Negro poets, to be sure! Do they not
> set the fashion, and give laws to the public taste? Let one of them,
> in the swamps of Carolina, compose a new song, and it no sooner
> reaches the ear of a white *amateur,* than it is written down,
> amended, (that is, almost spoilt,) printed, and then put upon a

course of rapid dissemination, to cease only with the utmost bounds of Anglo-Saxondom, perhaps of the world.[14]

Kennard's comments reveal much about antebellum popular culture, its ties to ideas of blackness, and prevailing attitudes of the era about race, class, and cultural nationalism. The most obvious signifier of these is his sarcastic concern regarding the encroachment of black culture on white culture. The classic tension between American low culture (the southern "swamps") and high culture ("the utmost bounds of Anglo-Saxondom") is evident, and the racial correlations of blackness and whiteness are clear. Second, he attributes an authenticity and a purity to black culture that have been used to characterize the popular. In his assumption that the dissemination and performance of black culture by whites has "spoilt" the true artifact of black culture, Kennard reveals his association of black "folk" with the authentic. Perhaps most interesting, as the scholar Robert Nowatzki notes, is the anxiety Kennard expresses about black culture coming to define a national culture. His exaggerated concerns are that the lowbrow marker of blackness will come to signify the whole of American expression—a notion his audience would find clearly outrageous—and that, more seriously, popular theater and literature have abandoned their ties to Anglo-European culture.[15] Kennard's sentiments are in response to a larger debate about the dependence of American poetry on European literary standards (one spawned by Ralph Waldo Emerson's famous 1844 essay "The Poet").[16]

The minstrel stage was, finally, a place where distinctions between highbrow (in this period meaning educated) and lowbrow (popular) poetry were drawn. In songs and end man sketches, minstrels claimed to be poets, comparing their verse skills or comically misciting the canon. Take, for example, this sketch from *The Boys of New York End Men's Joke Book,* a collection of minstrel material published in 1898.

Poet.

Johnson.—I believe you are a poet.

Ned.—Yes, sir, I am, and to prove it, name some subject you would like to hear me make a rhyme on.

John.—Well, the flowers of May.

Ned.—The flowers of May, ain't dey nice? The Johnny-jump-ups, hollycocks, roses, and de big sun-flowers. You want me to give you some on the flowers of May, so here goes:

The flowers of May,
They look so gay,
Around them we love to play—
I golly, don't we have lots of fun?

John.—Why, sir, that is no poetry.
Ned.—Well, I want you to give me a starter.
John.—Oh, I see. You wish me to commence the first two or three lines, and you will then continue to build from the foundation.
Ned.—Yes.
John.—Well, sir,

Suppose I should walk out some fine day,
And by chance did meet you on the way,
I asked you for the loan of a dollar,
You did comply with this wish of I,
What then would follow?

Ned.—I'd say good-bye, dollar; that is the last I will ever see of you.
John.—Why, that is no poetry.
Ned.—All right. I know it's more truth than poetry.[17]

The setup for the joke is, of course, that even though Ned and Johnson are versifying such common language and subjects would never be considered poetry in the educated, highbrow sense of the word: "Why, sir, that is no poetry." Other minstrel joke books and songbooks include sketches in which minstrels try to emulate or claim knowledge of Anglo-European canonical verse (e.g., that of the Romantic poet "Lord Berren") and comically fail. Such minstrel songbooks, joke books, and sheet music were mass produced and popular in white, middle-class homes as amusements. All of these facts indicate that as early as the antebellum period debate about what American poetry was and how it should be evaluated was taking place through popular entertainments that played on the tensions between highbrow and lowbrow culture, the working and the middle classes, and white and black cultural expression.

Kennard's commentary and the jokester's poetry reveal the specifically interracial contact, exchange, and debate involved in defining national popular expression. Eric Lott discusses blackface minstrelsy as such an interracial exchange, and his analysis lends an understanding of how blackness worked as a signifier for both white and black popular expression in antebellum America. Recent criticism on blackface performance, he argues, has for the most part been limited to two camps: those who see it somewhat positively as a resistant celebration of black folk culture under slavery and those who see it negatively as white performers' appropriation of black culture. Rather than aligning himself with either view, Lott acknowledges the contradictions and ambiguities of blackface performance, and looks to the systems of desire between its white working-class audiences and performers to understand the racial, gender, and class matrix of the 1830s and 1840s. He argues that blackface performance was a place for working-class whites to cross the color line and express identification with the black American condition while at the same time making African Americans the subjects of ridicule. This happened specifically through the representation of black male bodies onstage.

> The very form of blackface acts—an investiture in black bodies—seems a manifestation of the particular desire [of blackface performers] to try on the accents of "blackness" and demonstrates the permeability of the color line. . . . It was cross-racial desire that coupled a nearly insupportable fascination and a self-protective derision with respect to black people and their cultural practices, and that made blackface minstrelsy less a sign of absolute white power and control than of panic, anxiety, terror, pleasure.[18]

Lott dubs this ambivalent desire "love and theft": a "mixed economy of celebration and exploitation" embodied in the performance of black bodies, speech, language, and poetics by whites. This ambivalence also served to commodify black male bodies, black poetry, and black song, "which troubled guilty whites all the more because they were so attracted to the culture they plundered."[19] In making African Americans objects of ridicule and desire, minstrelsy's place among forms of popular expression not only signified a break between high and low culture but also signified the complexity of the cultural and political economy of America. The creation of national popular culture through minstrel performances was not limited to caricatures of African Americans; the scholar William Mahar notes that minstrel acts also included impersonations and caricatures of women, Jews, Italians, and the Irish.[20] Blackface performances were only the most popular and pervasive acts of these.

Minstrelsy's cross-racial exchange and cultural styles enabled a new bohemian literary aesthetic to emerge in the United States whose practitioners include Walt Whitman, Carl Van Vechten, and the Beats.[21] Originating in the Gypsy culture of mid-nineteenth-century France, bohemianism was characterized by a (sometimes rather vague) rebellion against society and the upper class. American bohemianism promoted individualism and favored the dramatic, turning Greenwich Village pubs into unlikely venues for art and literature.[22] Herein lay a new home for popular poetry, one in which difference and marginality were celebrated. Performances of blackness, Lott notes, helped encode this sense of bohemian marginality. Bohemian artists "immersed themselves in 'blackness' to indulge their felt sense of difference" and to gain "certain underground privileges," opening the door to "that fascinating imaginary space of fun and license outside (but structured by) Victorian bourgeois norms."[23] This sense of difference, liminality, and play—all enabled by performances of blackness—is a familiar strain in a much more recent popular poetry movement, the Beat movement. Bohemianism was both an inspiration for and a tenet of Beat culture, and it similarly used the signifier of blackness to achieve distance from academic and dominant culture in its era.

Bringing the "Cultural Dowry": Beat Poetry's Performances of Black Culture

As artists we were oppressed and indeed people of the nation were oppressed. . . . We saw that the art of poetry was essentially dead—killed by war, by academies, by neglect, by lack of love, and by disinterest. We knew we could bring it back to life.

    —Michael McClure, *Scratching the Beat Surface*

Postwar literature "for the people" in the late 1940s and 1950s took shape in Beat poetry and fiction. Beat writers, fueled by jazz, Benzedrine, and the American road, inspired rebellion and experimentation in a young generation of Americans, and they resisted the status quo established by both the academy and white, middle-class culture. In a 1961 essay, Beat poet Allen Ginsberg called the academy both "enemy and Philistine host" and threatened, "[P]retty soon I'm going to stop even trying to communicate coherently to the majority of the academic, journalistic, mass media, and publishing trade and leave them to stew in their own juice of ridiculous messy ideas. SQUARES SHUT UP and LEARN OR GO HOME."[24] Jack Kerouac was infamous for writing with what one author called "his antithetical approach to the sterility of the learned."[25]

The moniker *beat,* as it was used to define this generation of writers, encompassed many meanings, including "beatitude, beaten, beatific, beatnik, bohemian, and jazzy."[26] The term originated in black jazz culture, meaning "poor and exhausted," "broke and broken." This "hip language" filtered from jazz clubs to the heroin culture of the streets, and it was Herbert Hunke, a Times Square hustler, who introduced both the word and its companion narcotic to William Burroughs in 1944.[27] The term was soon taken up within Burroughs's circle of friends, which included Allen Ginsberg and Jack Kerouac. John Clellon Holmes, a friend of Kerouac, canonized the phrase "beat generation" in his 1952 *New York Times Magazine* article "This Is the Beat Generation," and by the late 1950s the term was being used to describe anyone leading a bohemian or rebellious lifestyle.[28]

For many Beats, the poetry reading was the key element defining the movement's novelty, rebellion, and popularity, and performance determined the composition, form, and content of their work. Performance space and setting also took beat poetry into a new realm. The scholar Lorenzo Thomas notes that Beat authors "were interested in resurrecting the poetry reading as something other than a genteel diversion,"[29] and to do so Beats took their readings into coffeehouses, bars, lofts, and cellars. These venues were distinctly and consciously separate from academic settings in order to encourage experimentation and reach nonacademic audiences. Later, when their literature had become recognized as a school of writing and they were invited to perform at academic venues, Beat poets often broke the unspoken rules of academic readings by inviting audience participation, employing instruments and music, and making the event more of a free-for-all than a solemn appreciation of the author.

Early Beat readings were often small, drunken, chaotic events, but they also established some of the conventions of today's poetry readings and slams. Open mic readings, for example, were instituted to allow new and young writers an opportunity to receive criticism in a welcoming atmosphere. Beat readings also allowed more women (such as Diane DiPrima) and people of color (such as LeRoi Jones) significant stage time, although white men unquestionably dominated the Beat spotlight.

What is regarded as the seminal Beat performance was an invitational reading at which Ginsberg performed his long poem *Howl* for the first time. The Six Gallery Reading, as it is now known, also featured Phillip Lamantia, Michael McClure, Gary Snyder, and Philip Whalen. The reading was the birth of Beat performance and set an example for both future readers and audience members. Ginsberg recalls:

> In the Fall of 1955 a group of six unknown poets in San Francisco, in a moment of drunken enthusiasm, decided to defy the system of academic poetry, official reviews, New York publishing machinery, national sobriety and generally accepted standards to good taste, by giving a free reading of their poetry in a run down second rate experimental art gallery in the Negro section of San Francisco. They sent out a hundred postcards, put up signs in North Beach (Latin Quarter) bars, bought a lot of wine to get the audience drunk, and invited the well-known Frisco Anarchist resident poet Kenneth Rexroth to act as Master of Ceremonies. Their approach was purely amateur and goofy, but it should be noted that they represented a remarkable lineup of experience and character—it was an assemblage of really good poets who knew what they were writing and didn't care about anything else. They got drunk, the audience got drunk, all that was missing was the orgy. This was no ordinary poetry reading. Indeed, it resembled anything but a poetry reading.[30]

This defiance of the typically stoic poetry reading would become characteristic of the Beats. In fact, this attitude is something Beat authors would come to perform at their events. It is interesting, then, that in defying the dominant literary culture Ginsberg made it a point to note that the Six Gallery was in "a Negro section of town" and the reading was advertised in North Beach. The choice to do so is one example of how the signifier of blackness was used by the Beats to distinguish their performances and aesthetics from those of the academy and white dominant culture. The attendees were also marked in this way through their jazz-inspired responses; Gregory Corso and Ginsberg note that audience member Kerouac "shout[ed] encouragement or respond[ed] with spontaneous images—jazz style—to the long zig-zag rhythms in *Howl*."[31] In these ways, the reading that would become the blueprint for other Beat readings exhibits black aesthetics while painting the readings of official verse culture as conspicuously white.[32]

Even in later years, when Beat readings eventually moved from hipster lofts to more traditional campus settings, these performances did not, as Bruce Cook notes, adopt a "solemn-occasion-sponsored-by-the-English-Department" tenor. Instead, "All those present participated: applauding, answering back, shouting encouragement."[33] The use of call-and-response, a tradition that originated in African American oratory, is one device Beats used to rouse audiences. Another critic described Beat audiences as "like Elvis Presley fans at a Rock and Roll binge, shouting stamping, whistling, doing snake dances in the aisles," behavior inspired by black blues culture and the performances of artists such as Presley who dared to cross the color line.[34] Such descriptions are evidence that Beat performance reflects a cultural dialectic between black and white artists and their audiences.

The late 1940s and 1950s proved a time of cultural anxiety for self-proclaimed subterranean artists who deemed themselves "hipsters," an anxiety shared by many artists of the period. The year 1947 heralded W. H. Auden's poem "The Age of Anxiety," which won the Pulitzer prize. Abstract expressionist painters such as Jackson Pollack, Philip Guston, and Mark Rothko indicated their discontent with Eisenhower era nationalism and optimism by funneling anxiety into their art and aesthetic discourses.[35] In music, cultural discontent was especially channeled through black performance. The popularity of black musical genres such as bebop and jazz among white youth caused anxiety over the strict racial boundaries common in their middle-class households, a phenomenon that made the token of blackness all the more attractive to white counterculturalists. Beat discontent stemmed from the perception of national public "crises" of consumerism, postwar national identity, political apathy, and middle-class ennui. It should come as no surprise that in seeking to resist dominant postwar culture—a desire stated nowhere more plainly than by Gregory Corso, who wrote that "by avoiding society you become separate from society and being separate from society is being beat"—many Beat hipsters expressed this resistance to mainstream culture through projections of blackness.[36]

By taking signifiers from the overlapping cultures of jazz and heroin—cultures that were, in the imagination of the white mainstream, strongly associated with black masculinity—Beat writers sought to inhabit what they saw as the social alienation of black males in the 1950s (an alienation famously portrayed in Ralph Ellison's novel *Invisible Man*). Stephen Henderson, writing about the Black Arts movement in 1973, remarks that "in effect, the Beats were approaching through empathy with the Black Experience some of the very same considerations—technical and thematic—that . . . the present generation of Black poets have approached from the *inside,* so to speak."[37] The Beats' preoccupation with and appropriation of black masculinity to remove themselves from mainstream culture (and it bears note that Beat attention was particularly focused on black men) proved to be somewhat misguided. For example, Beats argued for racial integration through black males' sexual domination of white women, an inversion of plantation-style miscegenation that Kenneth Rexroth called "Crow-Jimism." Other aspects of Beat authors' appropriations of blackness were similarly stereotypical and sexist; Werner Sollors notes that "whether imagined as a noble savage, exotic primitive, or a violent psychopath, the Beats' 'Negro' remained a projection, an inversion of earlier square, racist versions of the brute Negro. . . . For the sake of convenience, the Bohemian might call 'Negro' everything he thought white America unjustly repressed."[38] Blackness became an emblem of liminality, and Beat authors often used projections of black speech, music, and culture to perform their social alienation and literary "otherness." In this way, the performance of black signifiers became a way to negate and distance oneself from dominant white culture even as the artists were white themselves.

Norman Mailer's infamous 1959 essay "The White Negro" is the most outstanding example of this racial caricature. Despite its sexist and racist premises, the essay lends insight into how Beats viewed black culture and how Beat hipsters took on performative signifiers of blackness in order to rebel against dominant culture. The hipster, Mailer argues, is "a psychic outlaw" who lives in the existential shadow of the cold war. He uses the language of the street—lingo such as "cool," "with it," "crazy," "dig," and "square"—that had trickled down from jazz culture. Indeed, Mailer dubs the black jazzman "the cultural mentor" of hipsters.

This particular part of a generation was attracted to what the Negro had to offer. In such places as Greenwich Village, a ménage-a-trois was completed—the bohemian and the juvenile delinquent came face-to-face with the Negro, and the hipster was a fact of American life. If marijuana was the wedding ring, the child was the language of Hip for its argot gave expression to abstract states of feeling which all could share, at least all who were Hip. And in this wedding of the white and black it was the Negro who brought the cultural dowry.[39]

This cultural dowry, he continues, includes the "Negro's" sense of oppression, his survival despite the constant threat of violence, his connection to bodily pleasure and sexuality, his musicality, his psychopathology, and his seemingly innate connection to "the primitive."

Mailer's view of African American experience is unsurprisingly reductive but still telling. His essay posits that the Beat hipster adopts symbols of blackness and "absorb[s] the existentialist synapses of the Negro, and for practical purposes could be considered a white Negro."[40] Mailer makes it clear that blackness and black culture (or at least the caricature that he envisions blackness and black culture to signify) provide the illegitimately acquired knowledge that comprises hip.[41] His views suggest that it is black culture that fuels Beat poetry's sense of resistance to the academy and the white bourgeoisie, black language that bestows on Beat literature the rubric of the street, and the idea of blackness itself that lends Beat poetry its illegitimacy and hence its claim to the popular.

With the image of "the white Negro" specifically in mind, many have criticized Beat hipsters for appropriating black culture for their own purposes. In On the Road, Kerouac writes of "wishing I were a Negro, feeling that the best the white world had offered me was not enough ecstasy for me, not enough life, joy, kicks, darkness, music, not enough night."[42] Kerouac's fetishizing comments raise obvious suspicions about the sincerity of the Beats' investment in blackness. But, rather than dismissing such behavior as merely an appropriation of black culture and little else, I believe we can see it as evidence of the cultural dialectic between and across white and black cultures. That is, the Beats' performance of blackness is a sign of the material and psychic exchange across and between racial lines, although its expression is inappropriate by today's standards. It is in these kinds of transactions that, as Andrew Ross notes, "terms like 'imitation' are often read directly as 'theft' and 'appropriation'" and white-defined "authenticity" is mistakenly paired with black essentialisms such as "roots" and "soul."[43] Crossing the color line is a controversial act, but such exchanges between white and black culture are not necessarily politically detrimental except in the eyes of cultural purists. When done consciously and respectfully, these exchanges can often be productive in encouraging poets and their audiences to cross the color line themselves.

Crossing class boundaries was also important to the image of the Beat poet. Allen Ginsberg asserted that "the essence of the phrase 'beat generation' can be found in *On the Road* in another celebrated phrase, 'Everything belongs to me because I am poor.'"[44] Most Beat hipsters were raised in middle-class families, although they ascribed to a voluntary poverty. This poverty was adopted as a response to bourgeois consumerism and social conformity, and the hipster consciously projected an identification with the working class to convey a fantasy of removal from or transcendence of dominant, middle-class culture.[45]

By the 1960s, perhaps because of the burgeoning radicalism in the politics and culture of that era, the beatnik mentality had, ironically, been subsumed by dominant culture. Other artists took up poetry and performance in new ways to institute more radical countercultural goals. One of these artists, LeRoi Jones, sought a more direct and militant association between performance poetry and black culture. He eventually left the Beat movement over its appropriation of black culture and relative lack of political action and fathered a direct response to the Beats: the Black Arts movement. Assuming the name Amiri Baraka, Jones helped popular poetry gain favor not only among black authors but also, and perhaps more importantly, among black audiences through performance.

"Working Juju with the Word": Performance and the Black Arts Movement

Black writers do not write for white people and refuse to
be judged by them. . . . The poets and the playwrights are
especially articulate and especially relevant and speak directly to the people.
    —Stephen Henderson, "Survival Motion"

James Brown is the best poet we got, baby.
  —Larry Neal, "Black Writers Speak"

The Black Arts movement, which lasted in the United States from the mid-1960s to the early 1970s, was specifically geared toward reaching black communities and attracting black audiences. In April of 1965, Amiri Baraka and his cohorts opened the Black Arts Repertory Theatre/School (BART/S) in Harlem and laid the groundwork for the movement. Its goals were to address black audiences, celebrate the African American cultural tradition (known as the "black aesthetic"), and take poetry, drama, music, and visual art to the streets.[46] Although Baraka is the movement's most celebrated figure, a variety of artists and writers ascribed to its ideals, including Jayne Cortez, Charles Fuller, Nikki Giovanni, Haki Madhubuti (Don L. Lee), Larry Neal, Ishmael Reed, Sonia Sanchez, and James Stewart to name a few.

The artistic complement to the Black Power movement, Black Arts movement was decidedly antiwhite, antiacademic, and antibourgeois. Artists empowered their communities by addressing what the Black Arts scholar Harold Cruse called the "triple front": the culture, economic matters, and politics of black America.[47] The overt politicization of Black Arts literature often lent it a didactic and militant tone, which was enacted through performance. Indeed, living in a time of political upheaval in the United States characterized most acutely by the assassinations of Malcolm X and Martin Luther King Jr., Black Arts audiences were accustomed to and even demanded such a tone.[48] Like other American popular poetry movements, specific notions about blackness, class, and nationhood were performed to access and address "the people."

Because the Black Arts movement was based in New York City from its beginnings, one of the subjects reflected by these artists was black urban experience. Expropriating the notion of "the street" from white Beat poets, black artists such as Baraka fled Greenwich Village for Harlem and sought to represent black urban culture from their own perspectives.[49] For Black Arts practitioners, an association with the street was a strategic political gesture that gave African Americans room to explore their own vernacular and aesthetics. The street also served as the physical space for some Black Arts performances. As Baraka recalls his activities in Harlem during the summer of 1965, "[E]ach night our five units would go out into playgrounds, street corners, vacant lots, play streets, parks, bringing Black Art directly to the people."[50]

The audience these projects sought to reach was distinguished not only by race but also by class. As part of a self-proclaimed "mass art," Black Arts literature and performance were decidedly antibourgeois. In fact, the signifier of whiteness in Black Arts literature was often synonymous with the middle class; the Black Arts critic Stephen Henderson classified such literature as a "rejection of white middle-class values" and an "affirmation of black selfhood."[51] Black artists argued that African American writers of previous eras, particularly those of the Harlem Renaissance, were unduly influenced by white bourgeois standards and patrons.[52] The Black Arts movement linked race and class such that the black middle class (and literature produced by the black bourgeoisie) was deemed effectively white. Larry Neal argues that for this group "literature was just an afterthought, the step taken by the Negro bourgeoisie who desired acceptance on the white man's terms. And that is precisely why the literature has failed. It was the case of an elite addressing another elite."[53] For an artist to truly identify as black and to reflect black aesthetics, one had to identify as both urban and working class or underclass.

In addition to the Black Arts posture against dominant, white, middle-class culture, literary institutions and the academy were main targets of the movement. Baraka, for example, established BART/S with other artists so that students could learn the arts from a black, rather than an Anglo-European, point of view. Even in his Beat days, Baraka claimed to present a voice that was "commercial and popular against the academies" and mocked the "simplemindedness &/or immaturity of the official literary hierarchy."[54] There were, however, a handful of traditionally trained black scholars operating within the academy who adopted black aesthetics during the 1960s. These scholars—including Addison Gayle, Arna Bontemps, Stephen E. Henderson, and George Kent—were often the first to give serious critical attention to black artists.

What Black Arts practitioners hoped to gain by their polemical stance against the white-dominated academy was not only autonomy from white institutions but also autonomy from Anglo-European aesthetics and power. As James Stewart comments in 1968, "[W]e are misfits, estranged from the white cultural present. . . . [The black artist] cannot be 'successful' in any sense that has meaning in white critical evaluations. Nor can his work ever be called 'good' in any context or meaning that could make sense to that traditional critique."[55] The polemical rejection of literary criticism and the academy was an extension of the rejection of whiteness itself. Rather than relying on existing literary and artistic standards, Black Art practitioners turned to their own communities and experiences to evaluate their work, underlining a commitment to black working-class people.

Black Art poets undertook this commitment by writing explicitly on political topics and conveying their ideas through idiomatic language. This language was the same street idiom of black neighborhoods that the Beats had appropriated to define their hipster but one with a racially political slant. "We need a new language," the black activist Maulana Ron Karenga extolled, "to break the linguistic straight jacket of our masters."[56] This idiom quite consciously played black vernacular off high diction, and this formal resistance was reflected not only in speech but in print. Take, for example, these portions of Baraka's 1969 poem "Black Art," which serves as an ars poetica for the movement.

> We want "poems that kill."
> Assassin poems, Poems that shoot
> guns. Poems that wrestle cops into alleys
> and take their weapons leaving them dead
> with tongues pulled out and sent to Ireland. Knockoff
> poems for dope selling wops or slick halfwhite
> politicians Airplane poems, rrrrrrrrrrrrrrrr
> rrrrrrrrrrrrrr . . . tuhtuhtuhtuhtuhtuhtuhtuhtuh
> . . . rrrrrrrrrrrrrrrr . . . Setting fire and death to
> whities ass. Look at the Liberal
> Spokesman for the jews clutch his throat . . .
>
> . . . .
>
> We want a black poem. And a
> Black World.
> Let the world be a Black Poem
> And Let All Black People Speak This Poem
> Silently
> or LOUD[57]

Baraka's poem—or performative "score," as Stephen Henderson would call it—owes much to the influence of white writers, in particular William Carlos Williams and Charles Olson, whose forays into projective verse Baraka came to appreciate in Beat circles.[58] Many of Baraka's poems borrow an avant-garde orthography and typography from these authors (such as capitalization or lack of capitalization of certain words; abbreviations for common words such as *would, could, though,* and *your;* ampersands; and spacing within and between lines), conventions that several Black Arts poets subsequently practiced. What is also apparent from the poem's language is that it is written idiomatically and meant to be spoken aloud for an audience. Like a radio play, Baraka's poem is alive with textual cues ("rrrrrrrrrrrrrrrr," "LOUD") that indicate how the poem might be performed. In this way, Baraka's text shares the scriptlike quality of work by Allen Ginsberg and Vachel Lindsay.

While "Black Art" epitomizes the militant attitude of Black Arts poet-performers and their commitment to political activism, it also epitomizes some of these artists' prejudices. The blatant misogyny, homophobia, and anti-Semitism that surfaces in some Black Arts literature is indicative of the era and the influence of the Black Power movement, which often equated masculinity and heterosexuality with cultural freedom. Homosexuality is a consistent theme in Baraka's poetry and plays, and the gay man is often a source of ridicule and insult in his work. The anti-Semitic strain in some Black Arts poetry stems in part from the long-standing animosity between Jewish shop owners who profited off of African Americans in black urban communities; it also is common in the rhetoric of the Nation of Islam, which was quickly attracting followers in the 1960s as Malcolm X gained notoriety. The stereotype of the Jew became a symbol of the economic disparities between whites and blacks, and Jews have been historically reviled by some members of black communities.[59]

Many female poets, such as Mari Evans, Nikki Giovanni, Audre Lorde, Sonia Sanchez, and later in her career Gwendolyn Brooks, gained praise within and outside of the Black Arts movement despite, as Henry Louis Gates Jr. and Nellie McKay put it, the "paramilitary, social-realist bravado of male leaders in the Black Arts."[60] Their voices are proof that the ideals of feminism and black power are not mutually exclusive, and poems such as Evans's "I Am a Black Woman" or Brooks's "For My Sisters Who Kept Their Naturals" are powerful antidotes to the sexism that Baraka reflects in "Black Art." Still, none of these reasons excuse the biases that other Black Arts authors exercised in the name of racial advancement. Misogyny, homophobia, and anti-

Semitism have sometimes been unfortunate bedfellows of the Black Arts' militant stance, as Baraka's poem reflects.

Thinking of a poem as a script for performance instead of merely a textual entity is also a tenet of the Black Arts movement. Larry Neal argues how utterly unimportant textuality is to black poetry in his 1968 afterword to *Black Fire,* which is, ironically, the first collected Black Arts text.

> The dead forms taught most writers in white man's schools will have to be destroyed, or at best, radically altered. We can learn more about what poetry is by listening to the cadences in Malcolm's speeches, than from most of Western poetics. Listen to James Brown scream. Ask yourself, then; Have you ever heard a Negro poet sing like that? Of course not, because we have been tied to the texts, like most white poets. The text could be destroyed and no one would be hurt in the least by it.[61]

What Neal calls the "destruction of the text" is, according to Henderson, a rejection of the Western/classical emphasis on the permanence of the ideal form.[62] Black Art strove instead to be theatrical, ephemeral, and dialectic. Black Arts practitioners called art defined by its process, not its final object or artifact, "nonobjective."[63] By this definition, black artists reasoned, poetry existed not in textual form but in the dialectic between author and audience that happened in performance. A single Black Arts poem can vary in expression and meaning each time it is performed not only because of performative improvisation but also because of its reception by different audiences.

Through the medium of performance, Black Arts poets hoped to attract urban and working-class blacks, many of whom had strained relationships with poetry in a textual form. Haki Madhubuti (Don L. Lee) argued that the textual emphasis white institutions placed on poetry estranged the art from black communities and lives: "[T]he poetry on the page very seldom found its way into the home or neighborhood of the common black man, i.e., poetry in my home was as strange as money."[64] Furthermore, Black Arts writers sought to alter the image of poetry so that it would reflect and attract working-class and underclass black audiences. Rather than seeking legitimacy from white intellectual audiences, Black Arts writers worked to create and celebrate a "black mass audience" by, in the words of Gates and McKay, "self-consciously put[ting] a 'ceiling' on its intelligence."[65] The focus was not on "dumbing down" their literature but on developing a black literary vernacular, aesthetics, and performance style that these "masses" could relate to and appreciate. "Our contention is that if art is from the people, and for the people," Karenga writes, "there is no question of raising people to art or lowering art to the people, for they are one and the same thing."[66] In bringing poetry to the people, Black Arts poets performed their work in places where black working-class audiences could easily encounter it: community centers, bars, black churches, playgrounds, and on the streets of black neighborhoods.[67]

Black Arts scholars articulated the fundamental notion that performance, as a dialectical art, has the potential to be transformative and create political change. Their performances wrested the poetry reading from a bohemian happening or a reverent, polite recitation and treated it as an overtly political event. Black Arts poets such as Amiri Baraka turned to performance as a way to address the gap between literature and life; in performance, aesthetic protest and political protest could meet in a form that was accessible to African American audiences.[68] Early efforts of Black Arts intellectuals in the mid-1960s, such as those of the Umbra Poetry Group, the Muntu circle of Philadelphia, and BART/S, recognized performance as a means of connecting with the people. Larry Neal insists that

> the poet must become a performer, the way James Brown is a performer—loud, gaudy and racy. He must take his work where his people are: Harlem, Watts, Philadelphia, Chicago and the rural South. He must learn to embellish the context in which the work is executed; and, where possible, link the work to all usable aspects of music. For the context of the work is as important as the work itself. Poets must learn to sing, dance and chant their works, tearing into the substance of their individual and collective experiences. We must make literature move people to a deeper understanding of what this thing is about, be a kind of priest, a black magician, working juju with the word on the world.[69]

Cultivating a set of black aesthetics meant, as Neal powerfully asserts, cultivating a black performance style for poetry, one that married black performance traditions with a more current urban realism. Black Arts poets combined street argot, Western African vocabulary, percussive sounds and rhythms, call-and-response, singing, scat, first-person address, rapid diction and repetition, allusions to African spirituality, and the black preacher's aura to influence the direction of black popular expression.[70] Indeed, the work of Black Arts icons Gil-Scott Heron and the Last Poets, which teetered on the border of poetry and music, set the stage for the performance styles of rap. As exemplified by the sound of Baraka's airplane in "Black Art," Black Arts poets came to use sound and utterance as raw material. The kinship Black Arts performance poetry has with music is characteristic of the black aesthetic itself; like Neal, several critics refused to draw a clear line between poetry and music and indeed argued that they were one and the same.[71] In this sense, just as we would say music is a performative genre, Black Arts practitioners treated poetry as a performative genre and a popular one at that.

Finally, the Black Arts movement also asserted a distinct sense of black nationhood, one that, like the Beat movement, critiqued dominant white culture. Again, racial expression set the parameters of nationhood and took a combative stance against the white middle class. With roots in both Marcus Garvey's Back to Africa movement of the 1920s and the separatist notions of Malcolm X under the Nation of Islam, Black Arts practitioners rejected integration and believed that black people living in America constituted their own nation. Some Black Arts practitioners assumed Western African religion, vocabulary, or dress; others simply immersed themselves in African American communities and culture. These Afrocentric or separatist lifestyles were coined symbols of "black cultural nationalism."[72] Immersion in African and African American national culture, practitioners argued, was the key to self-definition and the practice of the black aesthetic in life as in literature. Addison Gayle remarks in a 1970 essay, "The Function of Literature at the Present Time," that "the idea of an egalitarian America belongs in the trash basket of history, and that concept of an American melting pot is one to which sane men no longer adhere. In the light of such realities, the literature of assimilationism belongs to the period of the dinosaur and mastodon."[73]

The practice of black cultural nationalism produced a new kind of black poetry—verse that was overtly political, used black language, used sound and performance in new ways, addressed both personal and current events, and dealt with the inequities many African Americans faced in the civil rights era. In short, it was avant-garde literature with racial and national foci. Strangely enough, it was an avant-gardism that was also populist in nature; the poetry, while experimental in form and style, was generally well received by working-class black audiences.[74]

Finally, one must also consider how Black Arts poetry thrived through certain performances of blackness—performances that, though rooted in the experience of African Americans, nonetheless were also performances of identity. The expressions of antiwhite, antigay, and hypermasculine sentiment proved to be divisive hallmarks of some Black Arts practitioners. The literary scholar Phillip Brian Harper notes that Black Arts poets' antiwhite sentiment—specifically as it is performed through a masculinist, heterosexist authority—served two distinct purposes. The first was to linguistically perform the interracial fantasy of annihilating one's oppressor, an explicit aim we see carried out in Baraka's work. The other goal, Harper suggests, is to perform a specifically *intraracial* function between African Americans themselves. The racial signifier "black" was an emergent identity in the late 1960s and early 1970s. Just *African American* is the most widely accepted term today, *Negro* was the accepted racial designation at the time.[75] Self-identifying as "black" cast these artists in a countercultural light, and Black Arts practitioners' use of the term served to draw an immediate and irrevocable line between themselves and those identifying as "Negro." In this way, self-designating as a Black Arts poet also meant aligning oneself with or explicitly performing antiwhite sentiment. This performance, which threatened one audience (whites) for the purposes of another (African Americans identifying as Negroes), is what Harper calls the intention "to be *heard* by whites and *over*heard by blacks."[76] This mode of address is also evident in contemporary spoken word poetry, particularly in commercial arenas such as *Russell Simmons Presents Def Poetry* on the Home Box Office (HBO) network.

Conclusion: Popular Poetry's "Negotiations, Raids, and Compromises"

For each of these performance poetry movements that predate slam, projecting certain visions of blackness, class, and nation helped poets reach popular audiences. Since the Beat movement, the prevailing pro-jection of race and class has been a working-class or underclass black-ness that has also been particularly urban. Similarly, poets' allusions to nationhood—from addressing tensions over black citizenship in the 1860s to invoking the discourse of a black nation in the 1960s—have shaped popular poetry in performance. These performances not only resisted the dominant literary aesthetics of their times but also helped create audiences that would not otherwise listen to poetry by any definition. In attempting to reach the elusive and nebulous "people," Beat poets, Black Arts poets, and minstrel performers aligned popular verse with entertainment and performed ideas of blackness that served to engage tensions with academic and dominant cultures.

This association with the people has also become a synonym for a more authentic voice than what literary standards or dominant culture allowed. For Beats, the performance of poetry had to have, in the words of Lee Hudson, "directness, surface feeling, *truth,* and simplicity. . . . [P]oets tried to avoid the stylized *phony* techniques frequently demon-strated by actors and the mumbling uninvolved deathbed tones associ-ated with a poet reading his own works."[77] Poets of the Black Arts movement were specifically interested in legitimizing black vernacular language and themes as well as representing authentic expressions of African American identity (i.e., urban and working-class or underclass representations). The entire enterprise of blackface performance—and, by extension, the popular verse performed there—is wrapped up in the authentication of racial identity by popular audiences even as all in-volved knew of its counterfeit nature. This emphasis on authenticity is carried out in slam poetry, too, through the performance of marginal-ized identities, particularly black identity, on the slam stage.

In their appropriations and negotiations of blackness and nation across class and social boundaries, these historical performance poetry movements indicate something greater about popular verse and its con-texts. They suggest a pattern of expression and reception in U.S. per-formance poetry that may well indicate a problematic race-based dy-namic of authenticity at the center of American popular culture. One can easily call to mind the appropriations of white culture when it comes to black popular music, song, dance, and even fashion through-out the twentieth century and into the twenty-first. In discussing popu-lar music in the 1950s, Andrew Ross theorizes that this recurring en-counter between black artists and white patrons had, in part, governed social and cultural relations in the world of musical entertainment ever since the first minstrel shows over a century before. Consequently, questions about imitation, and (the romanticizing of) authenticity . . . are also part and parcel of the long transactional history of white responses to black culture, of black counter-responses, and of further countless and often traceless negotiations, tradings, raids, compromises.[78]

In its appeal to popular audiences, American performance poetry also bears signs of this cultural negotiation. Slam poets, in particular, share much with the performance poets that came before them: they employ live performance, gather at nontraditional venues, express attitudes of political resistance, exercise ideals of nationhood and democracy, and proclaim marginality from dominant and official verse cultures through the performance of identity. In the case of slam poetry, perhaps the pertinent question to ask is: what does this negotiation produce, and what can it reveal about the dynamics of race and identity in American popular verse today?

CHAPTER THREE

I Sing the Body Authentic

Slam Poetry and the Cultural Politics of Performing Identity

I am THICK
Like your Aunt Sarah's pound cake
Sweet, sweet, lip smacking sweet
Filled with sooo many enticing ingredients that
You never bother to ask about
Given that you only want to eat
SLOW DOWN BABY
Check the recipe
You might be allergic to the eggs, vanilla, flour,
Charisma, abstract eccentricity, power
And I don't want you to get sick

    —Sonya Renee, "THICK"

your
verses I subvert
my comebacks come quicker now
mouth opens wide with retorts
in defense of the inflections in my accent
in defense of the articulations of my cultural enunciations
in other words
I'm defending sounding like a damn Puerto Rican

    —Mayda Del Valle, "Tongue Tactics"

I want to be straight
because sometimes being gay is just too difficult;
I want to hold my lover's hand on the tourist fishing boat
kiss him at Sizzler
and make love in an airplane bathroom.
I want to be straight and revel in these pleasures;
I want to be straight and still sleep with men.

    —Ragan Fox, "To Be Straight"

As places where authorship is consciously performed, liberal political ideals are shared, and diversity is celebrated, poetry slams are venues where poets come to express themselves. When I say "express themselves," I mean more than "to say what's on their minds." A frequent mode of address at the National Poetry Slam is the identity poem, in which a poet performs specific aspects of identity for the audience. This is the case with the poets quoted in the epigraphs, Sonya Renee, Mayda del Valle, and Ragan Fox, who are performing empowered Africa American female, Boriqua, and gay male identities respectively. Such performances most frequently stem from categories of marginalized race, sexuality, and gender identities, but they also include those of region (as with the Trinidad and Tobago–born poet Lynne Procope), profession (as with the cop-poet Corbet Dean), class (as with poets Ray McNiece and Cristin O'Keefe Aptowicz, who grew up in working-class families), and intellectual persuasion (as with the host of the NPS nerd slam, Shappy Seasholtz, who boasts in his signature poem "I am the one who gave Darth Vader asthma").[1] For many slammers, poems that make an empowered declaration of marginalized identity and individuality are a staple of one's slam repertoire. The poets and poems that appear here are iconic and well recognized in the National Poetry Slam community for their expressions of identity.

The increasing frequency of identity poems performed at recent National Poetry Slams caused one veteran of the scene to note the progression of slam "from a lyrical collaborative art to that of an art of self-proclamation."[2] A great deal of the work that appears in recent slam anthologies and films confirms the trend of proclaiming one's identity for an audience. This highly subjective stance resonates with the poetry slam's rejection of a New Critical objectivity or academic universality. Poets' proclamations of marginalized identities on the slam stage are articulations of diversity performed in resistance to the (somewhat exaggerated) homogeneity of official verse culture.

Slam poetry's emphasis on identity also stems from its embodiment by its authors. The performance of marginalized identity on the national slam stage is an extension of slam poetry's performance of authorship. As dictated by the NPS rules, poets can only perform work they have authored in individual competition. Inhabiting the space where the "I" of the page translates quite seamlessly to the "I" of the stage, the author comes to embody declarations about personal experience in performance. This is true even in the case of persona poetry and poetry written in the second or third person, for the act of live performance still hinges on the author's body and its visible markers. The author's physical presence ensures that certain aspects of his or her identity are rendered visible as they are performed in and through the body, particularly race and gender but extending to class, sexuality, and even regionality. Embodied aspects of identity provide lenses through which an audience receives a poem, sometimes causing a dramatic shift in the poem's meaning and effect, as is the case when Patricia Smith, an African American woman, performs a poem in the voice of a white male skinhead. As this example suggests, slam poets are not necessarily bound to perform identities easily rendered by the their skin colors and physical markers of gender, although many often do.

This practice also has to do with another important quality of slam poetry: its goal of achieving authenticity in the eyes of its audience. In striving for an intimate, authentic connection with an audience, slam poets lay themselves bare, writing personally empowering declarations like Renee's, del Valle's, or Fox's. The craft and execution of that declaration is just as important as the statement itself, which is to say that *how* slam poets perform their identities is just as important as *what* they say about their identities. Performance, as one might expect in a judged, hybrid genre such as slam, is the instrument that makes a poem ring true or false with any given audience. Although authenticity itself is a fallacy—the result of constructed, culturally sanctioned performances over time—it still has very tangible results in everyday practice, especially in slam competition, where audience members are charged with the task of evaluating lyrical performances of identity onstage.[3]

The preponderance of identity poems at slams may make slam poets appear as a rather vain group of wordsmiths—an accusation that is not entirely false. Nevertheless, slam audiences are enthusiastic about and seem to receive pleasure from affirming such identities. Just as slam poets celebrate their diversity as a group, audiences come to see these declarations and celebrate the diverse identities of the poets, creating a liberal sociopolitical space where the values of dominant culture are suspended and poets in traditionally oppressed groups are encouraged. This encouragement is expressed through audience applause; it is also, as a way to assign value to marginalized voices, expressed through judges' scores.

In the instructions distributed at the National Poetry Slam, judges are asked to consider assigning scores based on both text and performance (see appendix, document 3).[4] However, the subjective process of judging is often guided by a more specific imperative. "[T]he criterion for slam success," Maria Damon writes, "seems to be some kind of 'realness'—authenticity . . . that effects a 'felt change of consciousness' on the part of the listener."[5] This "felt change of consciousness" is indeed a powerful element in any kind of poetry, textual or performed. Ron Silliman notes that a reader/listener's sense of realization "occurs throughout all forms of literature" but is most amplified "through the poem as confession of lived experience, the (mostly) free verse presentation of sincerity and authenticity" embodied in live events such as poetry slams.[6]

Such comments suggest an intimate and important correlation between the performance of identity at poetry slams and the felt effect of authenticity. If the identities poets express in performance are taken as their identities in life, then many audience members are evaluating not only one's writing and performance of a poem but also the scripting and performance of one's identity. If authenticity is, as Damon argues, the main criterion of slam success, then convincing audience members of the authenticity of one's identity is a major component of a poet's success in the slam. This can happen even when the poem at hand is not an outright declaration of identity, for poets perform their identities at slams through voice, gesture, dress, and physical appearance even when they are not doing so through their words.

When considering the techniques, subjects, and strategies of National Poetry Slam winners, it becomes quickly apparent that not all identities are created equally authentic in the eyes of national slam audiences. More often than not, marginalized gender, sexual, and racial identities are celebrated at poetry slams, and performances of African American identities are especially rewarded. The National Poetry Slam community itself is overtly concerned with the expression of racial, gender, and sexual difference in its ranks. For over a decade at the NPS, readings specifically showcasing Asian American, African American, Native American, Latino, female, and queer poets have been held in addition to the regular bouts. Most recently, self-proclaimed "nerds" have also claimed their place in slam's smorgasbord of marginalized identities. Over the last few years, the NPS has sponsored a "nerd slam" featuring poets reading about everything from the Heisenberg Uncertainty Principle to *Star Wars*. This, it should be noted, is the one NPS-designated event in which straight white men claim a marginalized identity. The showcase readings are the best attended events outside of the competition itself, indicating that the performance of marginalized identities is an important aspect of the slam movement.

The liberal and well-meaning concern with difference represented by most of these readings (with the notable exception of the nerd slam) unconsciously reifies the positions of whiteness, straightness, and maleness as the norm, as not worthy of attention, investigation, or showcasing beyond the usual competition. These events could very well be a deployment of "strategic essentialism"—what Gayatri Spivak has outlined as the intentional use of essentialist identities to deconstruct existing systems of power—but the use of this strategy should not preclude its investigation.[7] This use of strategic essentialism, if that is indeed what it is, yields an ambivalent position for poets: the readings provide an opportunity for the celebration of these identities while, on the other hand, confirming (and perhaps even advocating) their marginality from dominant culture. Such featured readings mark these voices as fetishes, deemed to be outside of dominant culture while also being valorized as ideal.[8]

Proclamations of marginalized identities undoubtedly attract slam audiences, who may see poetry slams not only as literary or performative but ultimately as political events. With Damon's observations about authenticity in mind, it seems pertinent to ask why marginalized identity, and particularly black identity, is so often awarded the badge of authenticity at poetry slams. To fully address this question, one must consider both the specific expressions of identity at poetry slams and the larger cultural politics of identity that influences slam reception. Considering slam poetry through the lens of performance theory can reveal new understandings about the desires enacted between the author and audience at poetry slams, as well as how the authenticity of marginalized identities is not just affirmed but *created* through slam performance.

Declarations of marginalized identity and accompanying invectives against prejudice have become a chestnut at poetry slams, a somewhat "formulaic rage"—to borrow the words of John McWhorter—that audiences have come to expect and appreciate in a form of well-meaning, politically motivated support for marginalized people in American culture.[9] Although admirable expressions of protest, such poems do little to investigate the boundaries of identity itself; on the whole, they are more invested in articulating a common narrative of oppression. Yet some slam poets, recognizing the limitations of this narrative, take performing marginalized identity as their subject, yielding through parody and persona a rich counternarrative regarding the relationship between slam poets and audiences while critiquing essentialist notions of identity as a fixed entity. In this way, even as such poetry never seems to be free of its reliance on performances of authenticity, some performances of marginalized identity innovatively flip the common script of oppression, creating new spaces for identity's possibility, investigation, and play.

To Be Real: Performativity and the Authentic Self

When used in reference to identity, the term *authentic* applied in everyday use is often meant to suggest instances in which subjectivity and identity are generated beyond or without external (i.e., cultural or discursive) constraints. That is, an authentic expression of the self is often treated as original, unique, and reflective of a deeply true internal substance. For an audience to deem the performance of an identity authentic is to assume there is an original or essential self that one can perfectly emulate in performance. This appears to be a criterion at work when slam judges score poems, and, indeed, it might be the primary criterion slam poets have in mind when they write their poems: to impart some truth about their subjective experiences that artfully reveals an authentic self.

Challenging this concept of the authentic self, theorists in theater, performance studies, anthropology, and philosophy have recently argued for understanding identity as a social and cultural construction, one created by both conscious and unconscious performances in everyday life. As the performance studies scholar Elin Diamond puts it, "In the sense that the 'I' has no interior or core identity, 'I' must always enunciate itself: there is only a performance of a self, not an external representation of an interior truth."[10] The theater scholar Erving Goffman and the philosopher Judith Butler both refer to the presentation of self to others—the public expression of identity—as a product of performance. Goffman, in his 1959 monograph *The Presentation of Self in Everyday Life,* clearly addresses this issue of the performed self in his concluding comments.

A correctly staged and performed scene leads the audience to impute a self to a performed character, but this imputation—this self—is a *product* of a scene that comes off, and is not the *cause* of it. The self, then, as performed character, is not an organic thing

that has a specific location . . . ; it is a dramatic effect arising dif-
fusely from a scene that is presented, and the characteristic issue,
the crucial concern, is whether it will be credited or discredited.[11]

Goffman, using theater as a metaphor for social interaction, is talking
about the "performed scenes" of everyday life, not just those of the
stage proper, and notes that these everyday performances are sites of
identity production not identity reflection. To state it differently, the interactions one has with various audiences (e.g., a boss with an em-
ployee, a mother with her son, or a customer with a pharmacist) serve
to *generate* those very identities one performs (boss, mother, customer).
Goffman's last point about credibility is helpful in understanding the
important role an audience plays in constructing identity. Selfhood is
constituted by how a performance of identity is received and judged by
others, and so, in crediting or discrediting a performance of identity, a
social audience helps to constitute or dispel one's sense of self in that
context. If an audience credits a performance of identity, the performer's presentation of self is recognized and confirmed as valid; if
not, the performer is rendered a poseur. The act of crediting or discrediting identities is precisely what occurs at many poetry slams: audiences judge poets, among other things, on the credibility (i.e., authenticity) of their performed identities.

Judith Butler's work confirms Goffman's view, suggesting that subjectivity is constructed through the repetition of social norms that she
calls "performative" acts. The term *performative* was coined by the lin-
guist J. L. Austin in *How to Do Things with Words* (1962) to describe
words that actually do what they say, speech acts such as the vow "I
do" uttered at marriage ceremonies.[12] Of late, however, the term *performative* has taken on varied definitions that have earned critical pur-
chase in many disciplines. Generally, most performance studies scholars agree that the term *performance* indicates a real-time theatrical act
and the term *performativity* indicates the discursive process of how
that identity came into being.[13] To choose a reductive but benign example, a performance of the identity of "teacher" might be played out on a
specific day in front of a specific group of students, and the performative nature of that identity might include how other teachers have be-
haved in the past, the credibility of the identity as it is performed by
this teacher, and the reception of the teacher's identity by the students.

Using the frameworks of phenomenology and Lacanian psychoanalysis, Butler's scholarship on performativity has highlighted the complex and highly intricate ways in which identity is constructed through one's citation of normative behavior.[14] However, this aspect of identity—the citation of past identity norms in order to construct one's own identity—is not always readily apparent to those involved in the transaction. In fact, performativity seeks to authoritatively conceal the very norms it repeats, making one's present display of identity both novel and law.[15] So, if a person effectively performs the identity of "woman" by convincingly walking and talking in ways that are historically coded as feminine, that person's femaleness and the female identity itself appear "natural," somehow prediscursive, even though both are constructed by behaviors repeated over time. Nevertheless, an identity in this scenario is being performed, and a performative history is being cited. In this way, everyday expressions of identity that appear obvious and unquestionable are repetitions of a concealed history of identifying behavior. Under Butler's model, identity is not biologically assigned but is something performed through one's behavior (as with Butler's main examples of gender and sexuality).

If identity is dependent on the judgments of an audience using behavioral norms as their guide, then how does one assert alternative expressions of self, identities that fall outside of these norms? In this paradigm of performance and reception, it may seem that the self has little autonomy from its context and audience. Butler's answer to the question of free will is to cite examples of identity play, particularly that of parody. Through the parody of identity norms, she argues, one can make visible the usually concealed process of that identity's history and citation (its performativity), bringing to light assumptions about identity and playfully deconstructing them. Such is the case with her example of drag balls in Harlem (as portrayed in Jennie Livingston's film *Paris Is Burning*), where drag queens mimic and parody specific portrayals of gender and class identity (such as the Wall Street businesswoman, male and female military personae, or the preppy "Town and Country" image) and are judged by peers on their "realness."[16] Through such parody, Butler argues, one can challenge the usual assumptions about gender, class, and heterosexuality, in turn challenging the status quo and creating subaltern identities in the process.[17] So, as in this example, it is often a negotiation of one's free will and the history of behavioral norms that influence how a performance of identity is received by its audience.

Viewing identity poems performed at poetry slams through the framework of performativity is enlightening. Audiences cannot judge slam poems about identity as "authentic" or "inauthentic" without having a model of norms to which they can compare that identity. If a slam poet performs a poem about being a black male, for example, those who judge that poem on the criterion of authenticity must compare that identity with other expressions of black masculinity that are familiar to them. If slam judges reward poets who are authentic in their performance of an identity, and if that authenticity is actually constructed through this process of reward, then the poetry slam itself is a representational practice that *authenticates* certain voices and identities. In short, through their system of audience reception and reward, poetry slams generate the very identities that poets and audiences expect to hear. They prove to be sites of negotiation between poet and audience where the performance of identity is judged for its success or failure (its authenticity or inauthenticity) in the world.

Such judgments about identity happen every day as one performs aspects of identity in any given social situation, and these performances construct our sense of cultural politics; they are, Diamond suggests, "cultural practices that conservatively reinscribe or passionately reinvent the ideas, symbols, and gestures that shape social life."[18] The unique aspect of the poetry slam is that identity is judged openly and publicly through competitive scoring. As such, slams have the potential to reveal disguised systems of desire and power that underlie the performance of identity in culture, and they also can serve as spaces where identity is challenged and refigured through play.

Slam Poetry and the Performance of Racial Identity

If the precedents set by National Poetry Slam rankings and the attitudes of slam poets are any indication, the performance of certain identities are more successful than the performance of others. The slammer Eirik Ott comments, "I love that . . . someone, anyone can get up on a stage and share their experiences of being gay or straight or black or white or Filipino or Latino or Vietnamese or transgendered or wussy boy or whatever, and folks will just leap to their feet in applause."[19] His comments suggest that slam poets and their audiences have, consciously or unconsciously, come to rely on marginalized identities as authentic narratives in and of themselves. That is, a poet performing a poem about a marginalized identity may gain the reward of authenticity not only for his or her writing and performance but also for the well-executed performance of a marginalized identity itself. Of course, authenticity is not automatically awarded to every performance of marginalized identity; not everyone can write and perform an identity poem well. But for those slam poets who can, the affirmation of marginalized identities along with the sense of empowerment and protest that accompanies such performances may be what it takes to put them in the winner's circle.

Slam veteran and performance artist Ragan Fox characterizes the reward of marginalized identity in slam poetry as an "uprising of sorts. It's a declaration from marginal voices that their experiences are important, salient, and deserving of documentation. These individuals are rewarded by judges, because the masses are hungry to learn about what they were not exposed to in text books." Still, he admits that not all marginalized voices are rewarded equally by slam audiences. The performance of a marginalized racial identity, he elaborates, can "trump" the performance of marginalized gender and sexual identities.

> Audiences are almost expected to affirm race but gender and sexuality are different balls of wax. I can't count the number of times I've heard racial identity poems that score well bashing women and queers. It's as if the claim to racial identity neutralizes homophobia and misogyny or audiences, by and large, are completely apathetic when it comes to gender and sexuality. . . . There seems to be a definite performative mechanism that is woven into the judging process and its *excessive* co-optation of a *certain kind* of liberalism.[20]

The most commonly rewarded of these racial identities at poetry slams, at least on a national level, is black identity. Much of the popular attention surrounding slam has gone to African American performers, and mainstream media sources have often focused on the genre's ties to the traditionally black art form of hip-hop in urban areas. Other recent media projects such as the feature-length film *Slam* and the current HBO series *Russell Simmons Presents Def Poetry* have presented slam poets to mainstream audiences alongside hip-hop artists and against the backdrop of black, underclass, and urban culture. Poetry

Slam, Incorporated—the national body governing the NPS–has resisted keeping track of its members' ethnicities because its membership is largely (and proudly) liberal, under forty, outspoken, and very politically sensitive. However, it is safe to say that the poetry slam community not only attracts more poets of color than the academic poetry community but that these poets are relatively more likely to find success and recognition on the slam scene. A canvass of one New York City slam venue over nine months revealed about 65 percent participation by poets of color; as the field narrowed to the venue's slam-off to determine a local team, almost 84 percent of the finalists were persons of color.[21] Although these percentages are particular to a specific urban region and venue, as well as the pool of talent available that year, poets' participation and success on a national level confirms this trend. Of the fifteen individual champions of the National Poetry Slam, all but six have been African American. Similarly, almost all of the four-person championship teams have included at least one African American member. In terms of strategy, slam poets consider it a liability if an NPS team does not showcase at least one poet of color in a bout, and it is not uncommon for strategy sessions to revolve around issues of identity representation as much as showcasing poems of a certain tone, craft, or message.

The demographics of the national slam audience may be one reason for this success. The audience for slam poetry on a national level has been and continues to be predominately white, liberal, and middle class. In an informal survey I conducted of slam poets and organizers across the United States, many reported that this group constituted the majority of their audiences on both the local and national levels, with a few notable exceptions such as the Nuyorican Poets Café. Michael Brown, a former slammaster at the Cantab Lounge in Boston, posits that the audiences of the National Poetry Slam are predominately white because of the location of the competitions and the "greater appeal of slam to white folks."[22] Recent National Poetry Slams have been held in Madison (2008), Austin (2007, 2006, 1998), Albuquerque (2005), Saint Louis (2004), Chicago (2003, 1999), Minneapolis (2002), Seattle (2001), and Providence (2000). Many of the slammers surveyed agreed that the Chicago venues had the most racially mixed audiences, but they also agreed that in general the national audience is overwhelmingly white. Speaking of the 1996 NPS in Portland, poet Corey Cokes put it more bluntly, describing the tournament's audience and judges as "lily white."[23] Former Chicago–Mental Graffiti team coach Krystal Ashe recalls an NPS bout in which five white, middle-class audience members were the only choices for judges. "Here I was, coaching a team with two Asians, a lesbian, and an African American, with judges that didn't even resemble my team's peers. . . . They were wearing Dockers and button-down shirts!"[24]

The appeal of slam to a white, liberal, middle-class demographic probably has several causes, including affordability and the location of some slam venues in coffeehouses and bars in white, middle-class neighborhoods. Slams also appeal to students and young people, who may be more liberal minded or receptive to countercultural messages. Some poetry slams take on the aesthetics of hip-hop, music traditionally targeted to younger audiences. Thus, although poetry slams have always been and continue to be open to anyone, slams have cultivated this more specific audience in practice.

The appeal of slam poetry to a white, middle-class audience, as well as its appeal to young audiences, may be one reason for the visibility and relative success of poets of color on the slam scene, especially if the phenomenon of authentic identity is a criterion for success. Just as we have seen in crossover markets for black popular music—particularly in hip-hop, where the call to "keep it real" has become a virtual cliché—this sense of authentic racial expression has proven popular among white, middle-class audiences. Such audiences may be equating performances of marginalized racial identity with what is authentic on the basis that something so distinctly different from or "other" than white, middle-class existence is cool, desirable, and more real or genuine. Furthermore, if audiences have come to hear poetry that is more "hip" than academic verse, they (perhaps unknowingly) seek an aesthetic that has roots in black music and culture.[25]

Finally, the countercultural tone adopted in many slam performances encourages political complaint and protest; indeed, many of the poems featured at recent NPS competitions are invectives against social inequities. One of the most common of these narratives is the invective against racial inequities. In this vein, the slam may serve as a rare opportunity for liberal, white, middle-class audiences to legitimately support poets of color who critique white positions of privilege. Rewarding these poets may be a way of showing support for antiracist attitudes, confirming members of the slam audience's own positions as liberal, rebellious, hip, and against the status quo. In the reward of racially based content, these audiences not only affirm and construct the identities of slam performers; they also affirm and construct identities for themselves. Because of slam's liberal leanings and system of public critique and reward, poets condemning racism may be applauded for their writing, performance, and message, but they may also be rewarded in part because the audience does not want to appear racist.

At best, this process of reward opens doors for interracial dialogues; at worst, it may be a method of assuaging "white liberal guilt." Both of these, along with judges' preferences about writing and delivery, play a part in determining a slam poet's score. The construction of identities, both of poets and audiences, must be acknowledged in order to fully understand the rewards of poetry slams and the desires embodied through them.

As an example of an African American identity poem that employs protest, consider the National Individual Slam champion Roger Bonair-Agard's "How Do We Spell Freedom," one of the poems he performed to win his 1999 title. The poem is of special interest because it is both a literal performance of black identity and a *reflection* on performances of African American identity in the 1970s and 1980s.

I

In 1970 I learned my alphabet
for the very first time
-          knew it by heart in 1971
A is for Africa
B is for Black
C is for culture and that's where it's at
my mother taught me that from the Weusi Alphabeti
            at a time when A was for apples in a country that
            grew mangoes
            and X for xylophone when I was learning
            how to play the steel pan
black wasn't popular
or even accepted then
            but I wore dashikis sent me from Nigeria
                super-fly suits; sky blue with the elbow patches
sent me from america

and sandals made by original rastafari before weed &
revolution needed fertilizer to grow
>   my mother rocked bright saffron saris

we were phat 20 years too early and a thousand miles
removed
my mother preached hard work
knowledge and how not to take shit
D is for Defense
E is for Economics

II

I wrote my first protest letter at the age of 3
to my grandfather
for calling me in out the front yard ·
spelling fuck you with an
>   f - o - r - k - U

put it under his pillow in the hope
>   it would blow up and burn his ear off at night
>   wanted to get started on this revolution thing

F is for Freedom

III

G is for Guns—we gotta get some
>   Weusi said

evolved into 1979 and a revolution with a changing face
>   * *bang bang boogie to the boogie*
>   *say up jump the boogie—let's rock—yuh don't stop*

black folk and brand names became entwined
we re-invented dance and made wheels roll
with a limp
Cuba had just told America he was Africa in Angola
K is for Kings
L is for Land—we gotta get it back

>   so we lost Jamaica to the IMF
>   Grenada to the marines
>   and Panama to Nancy Reagan

jherri curls became high top fades, became gumbies,
became caesars
as Michael Jackson moonwalked his way into a lighter
shade of pale
       my mother sent me to america–she said
"Go fix that!"

IV

K is for Kidnap
S is for Slavery   —Weusi explained

cool became buttah became phat
    we lost our focus and our way
just about the time
black folk outside the nation
discovered the dangers of pork
      so fat back became phat blacks
      pigtails became dredlocks
      and fades faded to bald
as Michael Jordan discovered the magic of a fadeaway
jumper
      and endorsements
X is for the niggah who's blind, deaf and dumb
      X him out—Weusi said
my mother told me I should re-write that
that X is for the nigga who needs to be re-educated
that a corporate job does not spell freedom
marry white doesn't mean racist flight
a democratic vote is not a revolutionary act
      and as long as there's a sweatshop in Jakarta
there is no difference
between Patrick Ewing and OJ Simpson

V

God gave Noah the rainbow sign
-     *said no more water; the fire next time*
J is for James Baldwin—next time is now

H is for Huey

N is for Nat Turner

T is for Tubman

M is for Malcolm, Mandela, Marley & Martin got shot

two weeks after he told black folk to boycott Coca-Cola

Jesse Jackson still scared of niggaz with a purpose

—and someone must learn to read the signs with me.[26]

Performed in Bonair-Agard's thick Trinidadian accent, this poem takes on a unique cadence and assonance. For an American audience, his speech may act as a performative cue for the "exoticness" of his Trinidadian upbringing. Furthermore, it can cause the slam audience to conflate his national/cultural identity with the topic of his poem, racial identity. His accent and subject matter, in this regard, may be the ultimate signifier of an authentic blackness—something a white audience can locate as "other" than itself.

When I speak of the exchanges between a black slam poet and his or her predominately white audience, such as the exchange Bonair-Agard initiates here, I do not mean to advocate the idea of whiteness as the opposite of blackness, although this concept may consciously function in the minds of some slam audience members. The concept of blackness as the opposite of whiteness is a troubling construction, one that can occlude the perspectives of other people of color and falsely place each concept at opposite ends of the spectrum. Still the *contrast* between concepts of whiteness and blackness as it is played out between slam poets and their audiences is a compelling one. If predominately white audiences are judging the authenticity of a marginalized identity in addition to composition and performance, then the strong advocacy of black identity may be one of the factors that they further reward precisely because black identity is so often portrayed in American culture as the most marginalized compared to a central white identity.

"How Do We Spell Freedom" is a stellar example of a slam poem about identity. Underscoring this is the refrain that Bonair-Agard usually adds at the end of his performance: "A is for Africa / B is for Black / C is for culture / and that's where *I'm* at." With this refrain stressing the first person, although the poem is truly about negotiating the expression of black identity at different periods in time and in different nations, there is also no doubt among Bonair-Agard's audience members that he is anything but authentically black as a result of this declaration and his confident, assured performance. To underscore this even further, the refrain emphasizes his location firmly inside an authentic blackness by pinpointing Africa as the center of black culture and identity. In addition, the poem implies that, although representations of race are fluid, African Americans who have been commodified—"phat blacks," "Michael Jordan," "Michael Jackson," and "black folk" in "brand names"—pale in comparison to his own articulation of black identity. Bonair-Agard offers a definition of blackness that is militant, proactive, revolutionary and can transcend commodification. Completing this image of blackness is Bonair-Agard's live presence: he is a tall, muscular man who at the time wore shoulder-length dreadlocks. All of these elements combined with a stellar memorized performance of a well-written poem serve to make the authenticity of Bonair-Agard's identity virtually unassailable.

Rewarding such writing and performance can benefit white liberal audiences: reward displaces them from being the target of the black poet's protest. That is, in appreciating the work of poets who proclaim racial identity, audience members might assuage the "white guilt" associated with such an expression. This is not to say that black slam poets are rewarded solely to assuage white guilt. On the contrary, such poetry is also appreciated and rewarded for the cultural positions of power that it confirms and denies, and it may serve as an affirmation of the need for cultural redress. In the case of "How Do We Spell Freedom," the performance of Pan-African blackness may be particularly successful with white audiences because it is expressed through a critique of black culture instead of an attack on white culture. Bonair-Agard's "revolution thing" is not threatening to a predominately white slam audience; rather, it invites them to support the "revolution" without implying a need for any action beyond their support. White audiences, in this case, can reward a construction of marginalized identity without having to recognize their own complicity in that construction.

Still, there exist on the slam stage plenty of direct critiques of white, middle-class privilege by poets of color. One such example is Gayle Danley's poem "Funeral Like Nixon's" in which she parodically proclaims her desire to be enshrined like the famous politician.

> I want a funeral like Nixon's
> no acne no smell

no fuck-ups
Barbara Bush on the front row

No memory
ass clean
butt wiped

Let me break this down for you:
you see
I just want to die like a white man

blameless
timeless
ageless[27]

To play up the humor of her poem, Danley performs "Funeral Like Nixon's" holding her head up high and looking down her nose at the audience, as if a state funeral were her inalienable right. Her proclamations, performed with an exaggerated air of entitlement, have the audience laughing at every turn. Danley, like Bonair-Agard, adds an unscripted coda to her performance, describing the white man's memory as "blameless," "timeless," and "ageless"—then pausing in all seriousness, looking at the ground, and quietly imparting "and softly." In her sudden shift from comedy to drama, from playful hyperbole to quiet seriousness, Danley creates an incredibly powerful effect, transforming a fun-loving parody of presidential stateliness to a serious critique of white male privilege with the performance of two words. Such a turn, it should be noted, is a common technique in slam performance. The turn is what is called a *volta* in the Italian sonnet—a shift in tone at a pre-scripted place in the poem. At the slam, turns are sometimes expressed as a "let me break it down for you" moment—a shift in the poem's performance, usually done toward the end—that is meant to reveal an epiphany or sense of truth.

In flipping the script of white male entitlement so effectively, Danley's poem encourages white audience members to investigate their own cultural privilege. At the same time, rewarding this poem allows them to positively recognize the author's *critique* of their own cultural positions, creating an antiracist identity for themselves. Such a dynamic confirms that constructions of whiteness/blackness, urban/suburban culture, and ghetto/bourgeois culture are much more intertwined and complex than they are represented to be in popular culture. This dynamic in slam performance and reception is reflective of the white middle class seeming fascination with black expression, as we often see in the cases of rap, blues, jazz, hip-hop, and R & B music, and as demonstrated by a number of American performance poetry movements that predate slam. Speaking of this black artist–white audience dynamic in rock and roll, Simon Frith remarks:

> The immediate aesthetic response to a performer is identity, and it is the difficulty of the relationship between black performer and white audience that lies at the heart of American popular culture—rock culture included; sympathy is a way of avoiding the issue. The power of black music is, after all, a form of black power . . . and the attraction of black music . . . lies in its danger, in its very *exclusion* of white fans from its cultural messages.[28]

White culture's fascination with black artists and expression has a deep-rooted and sordid history dating back, as Frith suggests, to "the relationship between black performance and white pleasure" embodied in slaves performing song and dance for their masters, "a pleasure tangled up with guilt."[29] Yet this sense of guilt, however vague or veiled, does not lessen the white pleasure attained from witnessing black performance or other performances of difference. Indeed, as one sees in the case of some slam performances, it may be heightened through a complex matrix of fascination with, alienation from, and desire for the "other."

Parody, Persona, and the Possibilities of Identity in Slam Poetry

Although most identity poems performed at slams seek to confirm the slam poet's identity in straightforward and sometimes narrow ways, others tap the potential to critically investigate the performance of identity on the slam stage. Bonair-Agard's poem does this partially by questioning the fads that defined blackness in certain eras. Other poets have chosen to parody the rhetoric of protest itself, as in Taylor Mali's "How to Write a Political Poem."

However it begins, it's gotta be loud
and then it's gotta get a little bit louder.
Because this is how you write a political poem
and how you deliver it with power.

Mix current events with platitudes of empowerment.
Wrap up in rhyme or r-r-r-r-rhyme it up in rap until it sounds
    true.

Glare until it sinks in.

Because somewhere in Florida, votes are still being counted.
I said somewhere in Florida, votes are still being counted!

See, that's the Hook, and you gotta have a Hook.
More than the look, it's the hook that is the most important part.
The hook has to hit and the hook's gotta fit.
Hook's gotta hit hard in the heart.

Because somewhere in Florida, votes are still being counted.

And Dick Cheney is peeing all over himself in spasmodic glee.
See what I did? Make fun of politicians, it's easy,
especially with Republicans
like Rudy Giuliani, Colin Powell, and . . . Al Gore.
Oooh—see what I did? I called Al Gore a Republican!
That must mean that my political sensibilities
are much more finely calibrated than yours.
Create fatuous juxtapositions of personalities and political
    philosophies
as if communism were the opposite of democracy,
as if we needed Darth Vader, not Ralph Nader.

Peep this: When I say "Call,"
you all say, "Response."

Call! Response! Call! Response! Call!

Amazing Grace, how sweet the—

Stop in the middle of a song that everyone knows and loves.
This will give your poem a sense of urgency.
Because there is always a sense of urgency in a political poem.

There is no time to waste!
Corruption doesn't have a curfew,
greed doesn't care what color you are
and the New York City Police Department
is filled with police officers! Who carry guns on their hips
and metal badges pinned over their hearts.
Injustice isn't injustice it's just in us as we are just in ice. Yeah!
That's the only alienation of this alien nation
in which you either fight for freedom
or else you are free and dumb! Yeah!

And even as I say this somewhere in Florida, votes are still being
counted.

And it makes me wanna . . . [beat boxing]

Because I have seen the disintegration of gentrification
and can speak with great articulation
about cosmic constellations, and atomic radiation.
I've seen D. W. Griffith's *Birth of a Nation*
but preferred *101 Dalmatians.*
Like a cross examination, I will give you the explanation
of why *Slamnation* is the ultimate manifestation
of poetic masturbation and egotistical ejaculation.

And maybe they are still counting votes somewhere in Florida,
but by the time you get to the end of the poem it won't matter
anymore.

Because all you have to do to end a political poem
is to get real quiet, close your eyes,
lower your voice, and end by saying:

the same line three times,
the same line three times,
the same line three times.[30]

Mali makes apparent many of the rhetorical techniques slammers
use to gain legitimacy and authenticity onstage—including call-and-response, repetition, sampling, rapping, beat boxing, and effusive
rhyme—all of which one can recognize from black popular music. With
his first lines, he also makes a more specific parody of a New York City

slam poetry venue, the Louder Arts' "A Little Bit Louder" reading series, which is known for such political expression. He even pokes fun
at slam poets' use of the dramatic turn—the "let me break it down for
you" moment—in the last two stanzas. At first glance, the poem may
seem cruel or jaded, especially coming from the mouth of a white,
wealthy poet such as Mali; however, when it is performed after an
evening of slam poetry proclaiming the very same "platitudes of empowerment" that this poem parodies, it is almost always welcomed
with laughter and high scores. Such parodies can enlighten by revealing the ways political expression is constructed and rewarded on the
slam stage.

Other slam poets have taken on the parody of racial identity. For example, Beau Sia, a Chinese American poet and actor based in Los Angeles, is famous for several poems that turn stereotypes of Asians as
docile and industrious on their ears. One such poem is "An Open Letter to the Entertainment Industry" in which Sia comically embodies
these stereotypes as they appear in music, television, and film. He addresses his audience as if he were an unemployed actor at a high-stakes
audition, as in this excerpt.

If you need a Chinese Jay-Z,
a Japanese Eminem,
or a Vietnamese
Backstreet Boys,
please consider me,
because I am all those things
and more.

I come from the house
that step n' fetchit built
and I will
broken English my way to sidekick status
if that's what's expected of me.

Make an Asian different strokes
and I'll walk around on my knees saying,
"Oh, what you talk about wirris?"
cuz
it's been 23 months and 14 days

since my art
has done anything for me,

and I would be noble
and toil on,
I swear I would,

live for the art and the art alone
and all that crapass,

but college loans are monthly up my ass,
my salmon teriyaki habit
is getting way out of control,
and
I want some motherfucking cable . . .

. . . .

But I'm not preaching. Nome siree, boss.[31]

When one sees the poem performed, there is no question about Sia's poetic intentions. His performance is parodic and emphatic, and his audience responds with uproarious laughter. He achieves a sense of parody through an over-the-top comedic performance—crossing his arms like homeboy when talking about Jay-Z, executing Backstreet Boys dance moves, walking on his knees and speaking exaggeratedly in broken English at key moments ("oh, what you talk about wirris?" and "Nome siree, boss"). These techniques are especially effective in a venue such as *Russell Simmons Presents Def Poetry* on HBO, where there are larger mainstream, commercial audiences to be had, perhaps even agents looking for fresh talent. In the slam setting, where Sia's reputation as an actor may be precede him, it is clear that this poem is an incisive critique of the roles Asians are offered in his profession. By exaggeratedly embodying stereotypes of racial identity, Sia innovatively transcends them, asking his audience to question their assumptions about and consumption of performances of racial identity.

Another example of the parody of race performance is Amalia Ortiz's poem "Chicana Poet." In the poem, Ortiz, who hails from San Antonio, Texas, writes in tropes she has heard repeated by other southwestern Chicano writers: mixing Spanish and English to create alliterative metaphors, using Spanish terms for food, such as *melones* and *pan dulce,* to create sexual innuendo, recounting stories of "gang-banger hermanitos" from the barrio, or speaking in vowel sounds such as "aaaaaaayyy," all to parodically discover that she, too, is a stereotypical "Chicana Poet."

> . . . I could be a Chicana Poet
> because I know my history
> and whip out allusion after allusion
> faster than Malinche
> can be malosa
> faster than Cortez
> can conquer
> faster than Frida
> can feel
>
> and I think I could be a Chicana Poet because . . .
> I have a spiritual side
>
> yes, I could pimp my culture
> use all the expected tools
> box myself even further into a stereotype
> of an old archetype I can't even remember[32]

In her performance, Ortiz speeds through the poem at a breakneck pace, alliteratively mixing languages and metaphors in her declaration of identity. When she speaks of spirituality, however, she pauses, makes the sign of the cross, puts her hands together in prayer, and says with feigned, deeply voiced gravitas, "I have a spiritual side," humor her audience quickly recognizes and applauds. Although her poem may read as a critique of religion on the page, it becomes clear in performance that her critique is not of Catholicism but of Latino writers' performance of spirituality as part of their identities. In parodically performing tropes commonly used by Latino poets both within and outside of the slam, Ortiz calls attention to how they embody racial stereotypes.

When this poem is performed at a slam, Ortiz also plays on a slam audience's expectations about how she will perform her Chicana identity. Her audience has heard this expression of ethnic identity before, perhaps that very evening, and so through her parody Ortiz challenges her audience to investigate their assumptions about identity performance on the slam stage. Dropping the humorous facade in yet another "let me break it down for you" moment, Ortiz directly addresses the audience in the poem's conclusion.

> but you don't really want to hear about me
> just see me do that Latino thing?
> I am Chicana
> I am a poet
> some people may never put the two together
>
> Me vale.[33]

In this final gesture, Ortiz attempts to strip away the affects of race writing and performance, consciously revealing a more authentic (but no less constructed) sense of self to her audience: that she is both Chicana and a poet but could care less if her audience perceives the two identities as convergent. In Butlerian fashion, Ortiz parodically embodies the stereotype to overturn it, challenging her audience with a wink and a nod. In enacting identity critique through parody, Ortiz still relies on one of the primary techniques of slam writing and performance: the authentic self laid bare, revealed. Savvy slam poets and audiences can recognize this moment and sense of authenticity as highly constructed.

Another way in which poets explore identity on the slam stage is through the persona poem. By taking on the voice of another person onstage, a slam poet must focus much more consciously on performing a different identity than his or her own. If the audience is not aware of the persona as distinct from the slam poet, then, as Ron Silliman notes, "the 'I' of the text and the 'I' of the person standing in front of the audience are peculiarly wedded. . . . [T]here is a claim for the equivalence of the two."[34] However, if the audience is clearly aware of the persona a poet has the opportunity to draw attention to identity's construction, negotiation, and play in slam performance.

The four-time National Poetry Slam individual champion Patricia Smith has performed several persona poems in national competition, the most daring of which is "Skinhead," in which she, an African American, takes on the voice of a white supremacist.

> I sit here and watch niggers take over my TV set,
> walking like kings up and down the sidewalks in my head,

walking like their fat black mamas *named* them freedom.
My shoulders tell me that ain't right.
So I move out into the sun where my beauty makes them lower
     their heads,
or into the night
with a lead pipe up my sleeve, a razor tucked in my boot.
I was born to make things right.[35]

When performing this poem, Smith stands solidly, almost muscularly, in front of the microphone and makes few movements. The tone of her speech is in line with her character's: aggressive and tinged with her subject's sense of anger against blacks. Smith reflects on this piece: "I wanted to understand a man who unconditionally hated what I was. . . . [W]hen I perform the poem, audiences are jolted by his voice coming from the mouth of a black woman."[36] The obvious contrast between this persona and the slam poet's visible race and gender identities can be shocking, and this clash can create a space for identity's critique and play. Of course, having a black female perform in a skinhead's voice has a unique effect on the audience; in fact, this exchange of voices would be awkward for many others to perform, at least at a slam. Such was the case when Taylor Mali performed this poem at a tribute reading at the 1998 NPS with Patricia Smith in the audience. Because Mali is visibly hailed as a white male himself, most of his audience could not readily recognize this voice as a persona and confused the supremacist's position with his own. Those who recognized the voice as a persona still felt the performance was socially inappropriate. In short, the audience balked. Such a reaction is evidence that Smith's embodiment of "Skinhead" is just as much a performance of her own identity as a black woman as it is of her persona's identity and views.

This poem's difference from many other identity pieces is that it makes the slam poet's construction and negotiation of identity overt. The end of the poem makes this purpose abundantly clear by asking audience members to consider the nation's support—and perhaps their own implicit support—of the skinhead's views on race.

I'm riding the top rung of the perfect race,
my face scraped pink and brilliant.
I'm your baby, America, your boy,
drunk on my own spit, I am goddamned fuckin' beautiful.

And I was born

and raised

right here.[37]

In performance, Smith makes an unscripted addition to her poem, pausing dramatically after "I was born / and raised" and tossing her head back in malicious laughter, then dropping the amusement and saying "right here" with urgency and anger while pointing to the ground in front of her. The addition is slight, but it immediately and effectively puts her own identity and the skinhead's in sharp relief. It is as if Smith has chosen to speak the very last line in her own voice, suddenly driving home the nearness of the skinhead's threat. In another use of the dramatic turn in slam performance, audience members are offered a moment of revelation, and in this context they are confronted with their own implied complacency in allowing such prejudice to exist.

As individual political statements, identity poems can often be inspiring, enlightening, and empowering to their authors and audiences. But in a genre in which audiences reward identities they deem the most authentic, some poets may seek to write and perform poems that display their identities in ways that have proven most successful (i.e., as marginalized). The overall critique I offer here is of neither any one slam poet's expression of lived experience nor the quality of such an expression. My critique is of a cultural dynamic between predominately white, middle-class audiences and marginalized poets that rewards the performance of these identities as authentic based solely on their citation of difference, as well as the fetishistic desires that this dynamic can embody. The aspect of authenticity with which these audiences reward slam performers seems to veil the real issue at hand: the dynamics of power between poet and audience in the real world.

Still, slam poets continue to innovate from and improvise on the clichés that are reproduced in the slam genre regarding identity. Through parody and personae, slam poets have playfully exploited the expectations its national audience may have about marginalized people, flipping the script of identity stereotype. In doing so, these poets have created a space where the history of an identity is made visible and authenticity can be critiqued, permitting identity itself to be questioned and behavioral norms to be upended. Such work embodies the transformational possibilities of the moment between a slam poet and his or her audience—even as it may recapitulate the idea of the authentic self—because it questions identity as an artistic and cultural construction and provokes its audience to thought.

However, the vast majority of slam poetry does little to provoke this kind of thought about identity. Examples of well-meaning but ultimately simplistic recapitulations of marginalized identities abound on the national slam stage, earning slam poetry its stereotype as a series of angry invectives against oppression. As the work of Smith, Sia, and Ortiz demonstrates, slam poetry has a more nuanced narrative to offer about identity performance. And yet performances of the more straightforward expression of marginalized identities—particularly African American identities—have had the most success in making the transition from slam poetry to the commercial sphere of spoken word poetry. There, poets must negotiate a whole new host of issues, perhaps the most prominent of which is the commercial trafficking of black male voices and bodies in hip-hop music.

CHAPTER FOUR

"Commercial Niggas Like Me"

Spoken Word Poetry, Hip-Hop, and the Racial Politics of Going Mainstream

Over the years, many slam poets, including myself, have resisted commercial exploitation of the slam. Our reasoning was that the movement belongs to thousands of people worldwide; it would be unfair for any one slam or individual to capitalize on its name or popularity. But the door to commercialization is now wide open, and we can only wait and see what it will do to the slam and performance poetry.

—Marc Smith, "About Slam Poetry"

These niggas are honest as the day is long. They are commercial as the day is long. They are commercial niggas like me, and there's nothing wrong with that.

—Russell Simmons, in *Slam Planet,* speaking of the poets appearing in his *Def Poetry* projects

Although the slam proper began over twenty years ago at a grassroots level, national attention to slam poetry has been paid only in the last decade. This attention has manifested itself across several different media; representations of slam poetry have surfaced in theater and film, on CDs and MP3s, and on streaming video on the Internet, not to mention print and television sources such as the *New York Times,* the Cable News Network (CNN), *60 Minutes, Ms.,* and the *New Yorker.* Poetry slams have been featured in or been the focus of several feature-length movies (including *Fighting Words, Love Jones, Slam, Slamnation,* and *Slam Planet*). On television, slam poets have been featured on a short-lived Music Television (MTV) series, and the pilot for a slam-style spoken word game show, *Word,* was pitched to major television networks in the late 1990s. While these TV projects failed, HBO's *Russell Simmons Presents Def Poetry* series and Simmons's corresponding Broadway show have most recently found success in delivering poetry to mainstream audiences under the commercial rubric of "spoken word poetry." A distinct focus of many of these projects is on black performers and the ties of performance poetry to African American popular culture and music, particularly hip-hop.

Such spoken word projects are also indicative of slam poetry's current association with black culture and expression in the public mind. The fact that many newcomers to the poetry slam assume that it originated at the Nuyorican Poets Café—a venue that began as a safe space for urban Puerto Rican underclass poets and now is home to a number of urban African American poets of many classes working in the hip-hop idiom—is indicative of the widespread public image of slam having originated in nonwhite or hip-hop culture. This public image could not be further from the truth. Many new patrons of the slam are surprised to learn that its first venue was the Get Me High Lounge—a white, working-class Chicago barroom—and that its initial performances were rooted in the Anglo and European traditions of cabaret and Dadaist performance art rather than New York street culture.[1] Although several slam poets practice the aesthetics of hip-hop, the obfuscation of slam's Anglo-American origins is a symptom of its larger association with black identity and expression in the popular consciousness.

Given these connections between performance poetry, African American culture, and the commercial genre of hip-hop music circulating in mainstream culture—an audience that is multicultural but still dominated by a white, middle-class demographic—it is appropriate to ask how contemporary performance poetry is being marketed, reviewed, and consumed. How are African American poets taken to represent themselves and/or their communities in the commercial arena of spoken word poetry, and what are the politics of such representations? Who are the consumers of spoken word poetry and what desires might their consumption engender? How are these representations complicated by the commercial interests of production companies, marketers, recording labels, and the artists themselves? In short, what are the racial politics of slam poetry going mainstream?

The issue of representation is vexed for African American spoken word poets, as it is for many black artists operating in mainstream commercial venues. The scholar Kobena Mercer notes that because of the political nature of reclaiming blackness from the ashes of racism black artists are "burdened with a whole range of extra-artistic concerns precisely because . . . they are seen as 'representatives' who speak on behalf of, and are thus accountable to, their communities."[2] Like hip-hop artists, who are frequently called on or compelled to "represent" a neighborhood or African Americans in general through their music, black spoken word poets can similarly be called on to acknowledge their local and racial hailings.[3] As "representatives," these poets are often received as embodying the illusion of racial authenticity surrounding traditionally black language, gestures, situations, or themes, which can ultimately be limiting for both the artists and their work.

Still, media projects claiming to represent African American voices and culture engage a larger political method of cultural redress. Because African Americans have been excluded from many mainstream media outlets in the past, makers of these projects argue that black artists should be featured prominently or even exclusively, as the philosophy "for us, by us"—a trademark of the popular black clothing line FUBU, which reiterates W. E. B. DuBois's famous 1926 imperative for the production of black theater—suggests.[4] In the film *Slam,* for example, director Mark Levin set out to represent the plight of urban underclass black men in the American prison system through the fictional character of Ray, a poet slinging marijuana and rhymes in a Washington, D.C., ghetto. Russell Simmons's *Def Poetry* projects are similarly concerned with representing and promoting urban underclass African American poets; even as these projects feature a multicultural cast of poets, the vast majority hail from black and urban backgrounds (and of that segment most are men). In such venues, the political imperatives of racial representation—especially as they intersect with class and gender—can supersede issues of poetic quality or artistic merit. One poet auditioning for the HBO *Def Poetry* series reported being told by the production staff that poets would be selected on the bases first of ethnicity, second of gender, and only third of the quality of their poetry.

Recognizing that black identity, like all identities, is both performed and performative in nature, it is ultimately fluid. Performances of black identity by poets can take on multiple expressions and meanings, and, as such, the page, stage, and screen are all spaces of possibility. Still, representations of the black urban underclass in spoken word poetry are seemingly received by mainstream audiences as unquestionably authentic. On this issue, Wahneema Lubiano suggests that "the idea of authenticity—a notion that implies essence—can derive from the idea that a particular group and individual entities of the group can be recognized by the ways in which they are shown with some measure of the 'real' or authentic or essential qualities of that group."[5] The ghettocentricity of many spoken word projects shows how poverty and urbanity can easily become characteristic components of so-called authentic black culture when set in a commercial context.

Gender can also serve as such a characteristic component. Many reviewers of *Slam* suggest that black ghetto masculinity is what is recognizable, essential, real, or authentic about black identity, and this assumption is compelling. Although they represent a broader racial spectrum by featuring poets of many races, Russell Simmons's *Def Poetry* projects are also stages where black urban masculinity is performed and negotiated. Roughly two-thirds of the performers appearing on the HBO series are male, and of the African American performers about three-quarters are male. In the *Def Poetry Jam* Broadway show, despite a very diverse cast, black males were the most represented group. Almost all poets appearing in the *Def Poetry* projects testify to some politically conscious aspect of identity in their performances or reflect hip-hop aesthetics. Def poets who take up the negotiation of black male identity on the show commonly do so in poems about the high-rolling rapper, critiquing his greed and braggadocio in favor of the "truth" of the spoken word poet. As a result, there is a recurring conflation of urban black culture, masculinity, poverty, and authenticity in the *Def Poetry* and *Slam* projects—a conflation made by performers, filmmakers, film reviewers, and mainstream audiences alike—that fosters the illusion of an authentic black, urban, underclass expression free from the artificial trappings of commercialism.

The term *spoken word poetry* connotes several different kinds of work—beat poetry, hip-hop lyrics, coffeehouse musings, avant-garde performance literature—but I use it here quite specifically to indicate performance poetry that has strong associations with contemporary commercial media. Since today a poem's life as "spoken word poetry" is highly dependent on context, slam poetry can easily slide between the slam and spoken word camps, and many performers bill themselves as slam poets in the competitive arena and spoken word poets in commercial arenas. American audiences also frequently use the term today to indicate a hip-hop-infused lyric, and, although not all spoken word poetry reflects these aesthetics, in some cases spoken word poetry is indistinguishable from hip-hop save for its attention to political messages. This association is, no doubt, heavily influenced by those in the recording industry who are actively working to link one very lucrative recording category to another with untapped commercial potential.

Use of the term *spoken word* came about in the early twentieth century as a way to refer to the recorded, performed text of broadcast radio as opposed to written journalism and radio plays. When the National Academy of Recording Arts and Sciences established the Grammy Awards in 1958 to honor excellence in recording, they recognized this category officially by creating a Best Documentary or Spoken Word Performance award.[6] Over the years, the types of recordings recognized in this category have expanded to include a number of different kinds of recited and performed work, including speeches, journalistic essays, and audiobooks in addition to poetry, but what is most important to acknowledge here is that the term *spoken word* has, unbeknownst to many of its practitioners and consumers, commercial origins.

As it exists today, spoken word poetry is positioned at the nexus of hip-hop music and performance poetry and has proved to be a well-lit stage on which the tension between commercial and artistic interests play out through the lyric. Although arguments have been made for rap as heavily rhymed and metrical verse, spoken word has a more direct association with poetry in the minds of popular audiences. Spoken word, as the history of the term in the recording industry suggests, often seeks a commercial audience, and it is the rubric under which some poets successful on the national slam stage choose to direct their burgeoning careers. Other slam poets shirk the spoken word moniker; as the poet Ray McNiece puts it, spoken word is "a talent agency ad-man's camouflage of the P-word lest it drive away [the] audience in droves."[7] As he reflects, there is a divide in the national slam community about how or even if slam poets should pursue commercial success. Poets who do so are often accused by other slammers of "selling out."

From Gangsta to Poet: Hip-Hop and the Rise of Spoken Word Poetry

The stock-in-trade right now is truth, not the braggadocio,
keepin'-it-real sort of truth that has found its way,
artificially, into much of current hip-hop, but the all-
alone-with-your-feelings kind of truth found in poetry and
in the a capella works of rappers.

—Pat Craig, *Contra Costa Times*

As a commercial forebear of spoken word poetry and its current ally, black popular music can serve as a model for how spoken word poetry might be consumed as a mainstream commodity. The scholar S. Craig Watkins notes that "historically, black music genres that perform well on the pop music charts achieve greater market credibility and wider circulation because of the potentially lucrative sums of money white patronage can generate."[8] Thus, for an African American recording artist to go mainstream almost always entails gaining a white following. In music, this has meant appealing directly to white youth markets, which in turn has "provided the shaping context for greater social intercourse between black and white youth."[9] It also has led to accusations that entertainment executives are pimping black culture to white audiences, accusations that resonate as acutely today as they did in jazz culture half a century ago.

The most immediate and relevant commercial precursor to spoken word poetry is hip-hop music. The poet and filmmaker Jerry Quickley remarks, "The links between slam and much of hip-hop should be obvious, particularly on the business end of art. There is a developing shift within slam from art to commerce. That same shift happened long ago within hip-hop."[10] The image of the African American spoken word poet in popular culture emerged particularly in contrast to that of the gangsta rapper, whose music, also known as hard-core or thug rap, was popular with young white suburban audiences in the 1990s. This subgenre of hip-hop—which celebrates black criminality, promiscuity, misogyny, drug use, and ghetto violence—capitalized on a social climate in America in which black-white racial tensions ran high (characterized most dramatically by the riots that followed the verdict in the Rodney King case), projecting an urban black male criminality that white audiences seemed to both fear and revere. In the early 1990s, hip-hop labels took care to increase the marketability of rappers by advertising their street credentials. In more than one instance, this was achieved by peppering rappers' public relations campaigns with details about their criminal records.[11] Noted gangsta rappers include Ice T, Dr. Dre, and Schooly D.

The gangsta rap persona also arose at a crucial moment in hip-hop's commercial history, as rap moved more and more into the white mainstream. "For years now," Farai Chideya wrote in 1997, "the largest volume of hip-hop albums has been sold to white suburban kids. . . . The suburban rebellion—its record-buying tastes, its voyeurism of what too often it views as 'authentic black culture'—has contributed to the primacy of the gangsta-rap genre."[12] Gangsta rap vehemently disavowed white culture, and in many cases, such as N.W.A.'s "Fuck the Police," Ice T's "Straight Up Nigga," or Ice Cube's "Amerikkka's Most Wanted," it advocated violence against whites. This antiwhite sentiment only broadened gangsta rap's appeal to young suburban white males because of its association with counterculture, and in fact this sentiment became one of its most important selling points to popular audiences. As the *New Republic* critic David Samuels put it in 1991:

> Anti-white . . . rhymes are a shorthand way of defining one's opposition to the mainstream. Racism is reduced to fashion, by the rappers who use it and by the white audiences to whom such images appeal. What's significant here are not so much the intentions of artist and audience as a dynamic in which anti-Semitic slurs and black criminality correspond to "authenticity," and "authenticity" sells records.[13]

Rap music, Samuels further suggests, followed the fashion of becoming more racially exclusive, its subjects and styles more "closed" to white audiences and therefore more attractive to white audiences precisely because rap excluded them. In the 1990s, it was no secret among recording executives and artists that the more racially exclusive rap presented itself to be, the more "authentic" and hence desirable the thug sound and image became to white suburban audiences.

The popularity of the gangsta image across race and class divides during this period, Watkins postulates, made young, white, middle-class males the primary consumers of black cultural products. Their buying tastes spanned clothing, music, and film, all reflecting the thug image.[14] This newfound commercial success led to the production (and then the overproduction) of action movies dealing with black ghetto culture such as *Boyz N the Hood* (1991), *New Jack City* (1991), *Straight Out of Brooklyn* (1991), and *Menace II Society* (1993), many of which featured popular rap artists on their soundtracks or in starring roles. These products proved to be a way for the film industry to exploit the popularity of gangsta rap by seeking hip-hop's young, white, suburban audiences via their penchant for black urban criminality. Such films, Watkins argues, broadened the prospects of African American film production in the 1990s while at the same time limiting such film production to specific representations of "authentic" (i.e., male, urban, under-class, and criminal) black culture.[15] "Is there any life in black popular culture after ghettocentricity?" he asked in 1998. "In other words, as the gangsta motif loses its commercial viability, what is on the immediate horizon for black cultural and representational politics?"[16]

Exactly at that time, a new crossover image surfaced in mainstream U.S. media, one with its own pros and cons: the black spoken word poet. The popularity of this image owes a debt to the gangsta of the early 1990s for, although it is distinct from and often challenges the rapper's lifestyle and attitudes, the image of the black spoken word poet grows out of, and thereby often is iterated in reference to, the rapper's image. To be clear, much of what spoken word poetry does in commercial venues is point out the foibles and falsehoods of the rapper's lifestyle, and in this respect the two images would appear to rest at opposite ends of the spectrum. However, part of what lends black spoken word poets their authenticity is that they are fluid in the hip-hop idiom (i.e., they can flow). Quickley remarks, "To actually represent hip-hop flavor and styles within poetry, you must be able to represent, or rap, straight hip-hop. There are artists who claim to represent hip-hop poetry, and if they were ever caught in a cipher (a group of MCs flowing verse) they would be like the proverbial deer caught in a beat box's headlights."[17] Quickley emphasizes the virtuosity required for a spoken word poet operating in the hip-hop idiom to be considered authentic.

This is not to say that *all* African American spoken word artists reflect hip-hop aesthetics; some poets, such as Sonya Renee, DJ Renegade, and Regie Gibson, could be described as reflecting more traditional lyrical or jazz aesthetics. Nor is it to say that only black artists succeed in using the hip-hop idiom—in fact, the white artists Danny Hoch, Sage Francis, and Kevin Coval and the Asian American artist Dennis Kim (aka Denizen Kane) have achieved a good deal of success as hip-hop spoken word poets. Rather, this discussion is meant to suggest that black spoken word artists who reflect virtuosity in and between hip-hop and poetic idioms—artists such as Saul Williams, Sekou tha Misfit, Shihan, and Black Ice—may have a greater chance of achieving commercial success with young interracial and white middle-class audiences.

In contemporary media, producers, artists, and fans alike make subtle distinctions between the rapper and the spoken word poet operating in the hip-hop idiom. The first of these is in subject matter. In rap, particularly hard-core or more mainstream rap, there exists a distinct emphasis on materialism, wealth, womanizing, and criminal activity. Spoken word artists, however, generally promote matters of political consciousness or ethnic identity, actively discouraging racism and sexism.[18] Second, there are different lyrical emphases in rap and spoken word poetry. Fans of both genres acknowledge that rappers sometimes rely on trite rhymes and exhausted, unoriginal lyrics (e.g., "Put your hands in the air! Wave 'em like you just don't care!") to fit the rhythmic structure of the music, whereas in spoken word artists and audiences seem to pay more careful attention to originality of lyrical structure and content, with a distinct emphasis on message. Finally, the average rapper is seen as being motivated and controlled by material interests, while the spoken word poet is perceived as being inspired by grassroots political concerns.[19] In his book *The Dead Emcee Scrolls,* the spoken word poet Saul Williams sums up these differences in a direct challenge to "mainstream rappers."

> If you are in some way affiliated with any of these emcees getting airplay, or polluting your airspace with their lack of insight, I would advise you to begin reading aloud. Your shit will not last. You will manifest your truths and die in the face of them. These are your last days. We are growing tired of you. We love women for more than you have ever seen in them. We love hip-hop for more than you have ever used it for. We love ourselves, not for our possessions, but for the spirit that possesses us. . . . And we are coming to reclaim what is ours. The main stream: the ocean. The current. Our time is now. Word is bond.[20]

Still, it should be noted, the moral commitments and seeming "purity" of spoken word poets in all of these aspects directly augments their media images. Despite their differences, the rapper and the spoken word poet are identities performed in commercial arenas for commercial purposes, and certain aspects of these identities are emphasized in their media presentation to make them more marketable. Primary among these aspects are the falseness of the rapper's identity and the corresponding authenticity of the spoken word poet's. The contemporary appeal of a black spoken word poet reflecting hip-hop styles may be that he chooses to express himself using the language of hip-hop but within the venue of spoken word poetry, where braggadocio about sexual conquest, drugs, and ghetto violence are not only discouraged but critiqued in a play for cultural authenticity. In this respect, as commercial media portrays him (and it bears mention that the image is most often male), the black spoken word artist is often presented as the rapper reformed through poetic expression.

The African American rapper and his popularity with white audiences helped create a market for the African American spoken word poet, and the film, stage, and television industries have often used the discourses of black authenticity common to rap to make today's spoken word poet commercially viable in mainstream markets. *Slam,* Marc Levin's feature film about prison and black ghetto culture, and Russell Simmons's *Def Poetry* projects on cable television and Broadway are examples of this phenomenon. Both focus on images of "authentic" urban underclass blackness as expressed through spoken word poetry. These projects may be intended for, and indeed may reach, a racially diverse audience, but they also attract the white, middle-class audiences that are so crucial to mainstream commercial success.

Authenticity and Ghettocentricity in *Slam*

When we get back to New York and look at the footage, we realize it really can work. You can have a poet of Saul's caliber freestyling with hard-core bangers from the street; it isn't just a filmmaker's conceit. We study the ever-changing expressions on the prisoner's faces—the recognition, confusion and solidarity. It becomes our topography of truth.
    —Marc Levin, "Dispatches from the Front"

In the 1998 film *Slam,* director Marc Levin depicts slam poetry as an extension of an urban African American poetry community and offers it as an alternative to black underclass criminality. Throughout the film, the freedom represented by lyrical expression is offered as an alternative to the physical and mental imprisonment of African American males. The two main characters of the film, Ray Joshua and Lauren Bell, are played by poets Saul Williams and Sonja Sohn. Ray is a loner who peddles poetic bits of wisdom as he conducts small marijuana sales in a Washington, D.C., ghetto nicknamed "Dodge City." He is apprehended while fleeing the scene of a drive-by shooting and is incarcerated for narcotics possession. While inside, he turns his talent for crafting rap-like, spiritually conscious poetry into a response to prison violence. He comes to the attention of Lauren, an idealistic and outspoken young black woman, who teaches a poetry class in the prison and whose brother died as a result of ghetto violence.

When Ray makes bail and ponders the possible two-to-ten-year prison sentence that awaits him on his possession charge, Lauren invites him to a poetry reading and a romance ensues. After an explosive argument in which he reveals he is thinking about skipping bail, Ray meets Lauren at a poetry slam. She invites him onstage to read, and his poem about prison as the cultural memory of enslavement electrifies the audience. At the end, we are still uninformed about his decision regarding his plea to the charge. Instead, we are presented with a final nighttime scene that depicts Ray at the base of the ominous and brightly lit Washington Monument. This glowing monolith is meant to symbolize the white male institutional power he must face as a black man facing a prison sentence, and the screenplay leaves little doubt about the director's intention in this respect: "the endless white expanse of the monument, shooting up into the night sky, filling the screen . . . the nation's great white phallus."[21]

In their published diaries and artistic statements, the makers of *Slam* focus on representing the realities of the black urban male experience through spoken word poetry, in particular through the main character's poetic representation of (and ambivalence toward) gangsta-style crime and imprisonment. Reviews of the film seem driven to compare it to the "reality" and "authenticity" of black culture, in particular to the scripts of black masculinity and criminality. For whom are these images of the black spoken word poet being constructed, and for whom are the film's reviewers writing? Precise demographics of *Slam*'s audience are difficult to calculate, but the discourses of authenticity and realism used by the filmmakers and reviewers suggest that this image is geared toward liberal, white, middle-class audiences. A secondary audience is a black audience for whom black identity, social justice, and rap music are of interest, lending *Slam* an ambivalent representational nature.

Mired in the experience of prison, crime, and violence faced by many African American males in urban centers, Ray's role is crafted by the filmmakers to represent what they consider an authentic version of the black, urban, underclass male experience. One parent of this authenticity is the style of the film itself: the newly emergent mode of *drama vérité.* Like the French *cinema vérité* movement of the 1960s, *drama vérité* incorporates everyday people, situations, and dialogue into its film text at the discretion of the director, combining scripted performance with improvisation. Levin, discovering that his documentary shooting techniques were being picked up by "a lot of gritty fiction work, such as HBO's prison series Oz," collaborated with cinematographer Mark Benjamin to mix the possibilities of drama and documentary in *Slam.*[22] Their efforts resulted in *drama vérité:* a style that combines a loose script with improvised dialogue by its actors and real-life subjects.

Stylistically, *Slam* reveals its documentary origins through the use of documentary techniques, such as shooting with a handheld camera or using Hi-8 film (which adds a grainy, video-like texture to its subject). *Drama vérité's* "authenticity" also extends to its cast; although poet-actors were chosen for the lead roles, other spoken word poets act in secondary roles (such as Bonz Malone as the inmate Hopha and Beau Sia as the trust-fund kid Jimmy Huang), and several characters or extras are acted by prison inmates or ex-gang members. Finally, *drama vérité* also borrows the concept of real place from documentaries. As the second assistant cameraman John Kirby remarks, *Slam* was shot in the "*nonset* of the ghetto and the prison—genuine life locations as opposed to prefabricated sets" (see fig. 3).[23]

In describing how realism functions in British working-class, "kitchen sink" films of the late 1950s, Andrew Higson proposes that films invested in realism of a particular class are deeply invested in the exchange between surface realism—the sincerity of the characters or landscape portrayed—and moral realism—a "moral commitment to a particular set of social problems and solutions" around which a filmmaker organizes the film's style, narrative, and aesthetics.[24] Surface realism describes the physical accuracies of the landscape, acting, and mise-en-scène of the film, and moral realism pertains to the set of political interests a filmmaker conveys from the film's point of view. Transplanting these terms—surface and moral realism—to bear on *Slam* can be helpful in understanding how a version of black authenticity is constructed in the film as well as how that authenticity comes to represent a larger set of political and commercial objectives set by the filmmakers.

Although the narrative of Ray Joshua and Lauren Bell is fictional, filmic elements of *Slam,* such as real place and untrained actors, mingle to give the film a heightened surface realism. In fact, the style of *drama vérité* is directly invested in and constructs this realism, and,

FIG. 3. Ray Joshua, played by Saul Williams, pens poems outside a Washington, D.C., housing project in *Slam*. (Copyright 1998 by Trimark Pictures.)

like the genres of slam poetry, spoken word poetry, and hip-hop, it is not without its moral-political assertions about authenticity. *"Drama vérité* is the cinema of freedom; it is the filmed voice of real people," remarks Kirby. "Because of its populist method, [it] automatically stands opposed to hierarchy and rails against structures of class, race, and gender."[25] Like slam poetry, the surface realism of the film text complements its moral realism and vice versa. Its "gritty" style is indicative of a set of political values meant to challenge, provoke, and argue that the African American male is in a modern state of slavery.

In his production journal, director Levin asserts that his mission is to "tell stories that reveal the truth of our time. It isn't about movies, it's about life."[26] He also wonders if Williams, who received his MFA in drama from New York University's prestigious Tisch School of the Arts, can "be hard enough to pull off the street realism."[27] The anxiety Levin expresses about Williams's performance is telling. It reveals the film's imperative not to be only a representation of the cultural situation of black men in prison but also to reproduce an image of black urban underclass masculinity in its main character, an image that is "hard," thuglike, or otherwise authentically criminal. The negotiation of this criminal image with that of the morally conscious poet creates the arc for Williams's character and the film as a whole, and Levin wants to make sure that he and his audience read Williams as authentic in both roles.

Although it is soulful and musically textured, Williams's poetry set in the context of the film serves primarily as an extension of this authentic experience for the character of Ray and is the keystone for the controlling metaphor of slam as a physical and mental lockdown on urban black men. "i am that nigga," Ray proclaims in his final poem at the film's poetry slam; "my niggas are dying before their time / my niggas are serving unjust time / my niggas are dying because of time."[28] His statement "i am that nigga" is, to use J. L. Austin's term, performative in nature; it not only describes his identity but it creates his identity as black, urban, masculine, and self-defined in reclaiming and signifying on racist vocabulary.[29] Through his proclamation, Ray becomes the representative criminal black male that the film has made its moral focus even as he tries to signify on this identity through his poetry. The film's frequent articulation of violence and crime in this impoverished, urban, African American context—especially as it emphasizes "realness" and masculinity—ensures that such qualities will themselves, as scholar Phillip Brian Harper put it, "become incorporated as fundamental elements in presiding conceptions of authentic African American culture."[30]

For an independent film on a low budget (one million dollars) and done on spec, *Slam* has earned immense critical attention and praise.[31] Reviews of the film imply an audience of white liberal middle-class moviegoers who have an interest in independent cinema. In 1998, the film won both the Grand Jury Prize for Drama at the Sundance Film Festival and the award for Best Debut Film at the Cannes Film Festival. In review after review, *Slam* is praised for its insistent, authentic portrayal of the difficult choices presented to urban African American males by an antagonistic legal system. "The grit feels like real grit, not movie grit," remarks a *Houston Chronicle* reviewer, Jeff Millar, "and it's abrasive and nagging as grit is intended to be."[32] To whom would this subject feel gritty? Millar's language seems to imply that his audience would feel guilt ("nagging") and find the film's realism "abrasive," that is, antagonistically "other" than its own position. This, again, indicates a middle-class audience that is sympathetic to the concerns of under-class African Americans.

Just as telling is when reviewers criticize the film for moments when the realism falters, and these consistently coincide with places where the film text doesn't fit the "authentic" script of black masculine crimi-nality. The literary scholar Imani Wilson disparagingly remarks in the *Village Voice* that one of the film's "paramount fake moment[s]" is when Sonja Sohn appears before her prison poetry class—populated entirely by African American males—in a tank top, implying that the costuming disrupts the audience's expectations of the "real" (i.e., sexu-ally threatening or objectifying) black male prisoner.[33] Roger Ebert, in a lukewarm review of *Slam,* comments that the scenes shot in the ghetto and prison "were all filmed with realism" but that both the romance be-tween Ray and Lauren and the final poetry slam "seem out of another movie."[34] The film's criticism engages the many complex aspects of au-thenticity as it relates to black representation. As scholar Nicole Fleet-wood remarks in her discussion of youth, race, and visual culture, "Re-alness operates on multiple layers: as a concept alluding to that which is the essence of reality; as an aesthetic style in black popular cultural production, particularly of music and film; as a longing for that which exists outside of discourse; and as a set of visual tropes that constitute a particular racialized and gendered subjectification."[35] These multiple layers are themselves intertwined so that a discussion of one aspect of realness (in this case, the film's execution and aesthetic style) conjures another (larger race- and gender-specific visual tropes). Thus, although the reviewers' criticisms are first and foremost responses to the film's making, marketing, and style, they also signal an undercurrent of de-bate about the environments in which African American men can be read as authentic. They suggest that the film's best execution of the real is when it stays within the social and physical boundaries of impover-ished black neighborhoods and prison; when it escapes these settings, the stereotypical narrative of black urban masculinity does not survive and ceases to be "real."

Is this movie's commercial and critical success contingent on the sense of authenticity conjured by representations of black male crimi-nality? Further examples seems to suggest so. In *Slamnation,* the docu-mentary film that chronicles the 1996 National Poetry Slam, Saul Williams and his poetry are featured prominently. In *Slamnation,* audi-ences see two of the same poems featured in *Slam*—"Amethyst Rocks" and "Sha Clack Clack"—yet they are placed within the context of the National Poetry Slam and Williams's own life, not a "gritty," black, underclass neighborhood. Although *Slamnation* could most certainly be deemed to have more surface realism than *Slam* by virtue of its documentary footage (recognizing that a documentary is a constructed narrative as well), *Slamnation*'s distribution was limited to a small number of film festival circuits and cable network showings, and it never gained wide theatrical release. In contrast, *Slam* has been released in fifteen countries in addition to its mainstream release in the United States.[36] This suggests that mere surface realism is not the key to mainstream consumption. Rather, the release of these films seems on some level to be calibrated by whether or not they contain the moral realism of black urban underclass masculinity, the negotiation of criminal and poetic identities that engages the commercial legacies of hip-hop music and spoken word poetry.

An example of this is the caption printed on *Slam*'s promotional materials and video boxes next to a high-contrast photo of Saul Williams's face: "All in Line for a Slice of Devil Pie" (see fig. 4). The line appears nowhere in the film's music, poetry, or script; it appears only in the promotional material. For audiences not in the know, the curious caption may be interpreted as vilifying the film's protagonist and his situation, making them "evil" or "other." Indeed, "All in Line for a Slice of Devil Pie" seems to be a more suitable caption for a horror flick than a social drama. But the cover and its caption reveal *Slam*'s search for a certain demographic: audiences of hip-hop. The cover itself advertises new music by rappers such as Coolio, Q-Tip, and Busta Rhymes."Devil pie" is an obscure reference to a song not included in the film by African American rapper and R & B artist D'Angelo entitled "Devil's Pie," which critiques both the U.S. justice system and the gangsta lifestyle. The lyric might be displayed on the videos and DVDs of *Slam* because of the obvious overlap in subject matter and because Saul Williams and D'Angelo have collaborated in the past (Williams completed the liner notes of D'Angelo's 2000 album *Voodoo,* which features the song "Devil's Pie"). But the promotional trail goes on. "Devil's Pie" was featured in *Belly,* a film directed by the African American video auteur Hype Williams, which was released concurrently with *Slam*.[37] Billed as an "urban crime drama," *Belly* stars hip-hop artists in a black gangsta-style crime scenario.

What the marketing trail indicates is that the promoters of *Slam*

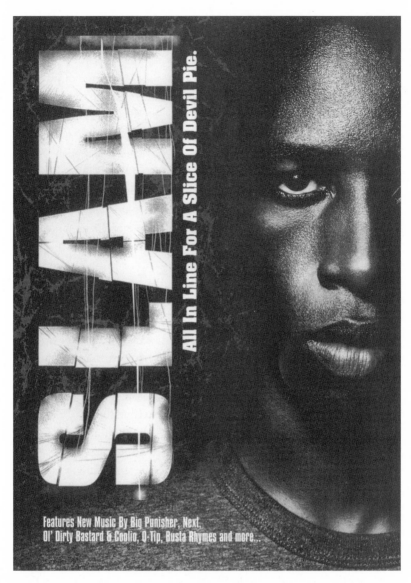

FIG. 4. "All In Line for a Slice of Devil Pie," the cover art on videos and DVDs of *Slam*. (Image courtesy of Lionsgate Films.)

were trying to attract a crossover audience from *Belly*—specifically, consumers of hip-hop. This gesture toward cross-marketing is indicative of the commercial links among black popular music, the authenticity espoused by this music (i.e., "keepin' it real"), and the image of the black spoken word poet in *Slam*. That is, to make *Slam* more marketable and expand its audience to include mainstream as well as independent film audiences its promoters may have relied on the image of the gangsta and the "authenticity" of his music and lifestyle. On the other hand, the use of the line from "Devil's Pie," given the lyrical thrust of the song, seems to be a clear *critique* of the gangsta's authenticity. In this way, it appears the marketers of *Slam* wished to cash in on the film's association with the gangsta image while at the same time putting forth an image of the gangsta's rehabilitation: the newer, "truer" image of the black spoken word poet. The product of such a strategy is a film whose protagonist has all the street credibility of the gangsta but none of the moral guilt associated with the gangsta's hard-core criminality and misogyny (Ray deals only marijuana, not "hard drugs," and rejects other materialist symbols of the gangsta lifestyle). As a virtuoso of hip-hop and poetry, drug-dealing Ray is an authentic representative of black male criminality while at the same time attempting to be morally pure by expressing himself through spoken word poetry. The interplay between the images of the gangsta and poet is something Saul Williams has carried out in his career as a spoken word artist. In a 2001 diary entry he recalls meeting Hype Williams and "think[ing] of the magazine cover I just read that says, 'DMX: Hip-hop's Hardest Rapper.' DMX was the star of *Belly*. If I were to figure into the rap equation, I'd probably be the softest."[38]

In *Outlaw Culture,* bell hooks asks us to critique "a cultural marketplace wherein blackness is commodified in such a way that fictive accounts of underclass black life in whatever setting may be more lauded, more marketable, than other visions because mainstream conservative audiences desire these images."[39] *Slam,* in its engagement with performativity, realism, and the illusion of black authenticity, continues to trouble and be troubled by the question of how to represent African Americans without encountering the dangers hooks suggests (albeit with liberal audiences as well). The politics of authenticity surrounding the reception of the African American spoken word poet can commodify black expression in very specific and limiting ways. By the same token, these politics can also bring attention to black voices and lend a complexity to black identity not often encountered in American popular culture. Audience members may indeed feel *Slam* is an accurate representation of a Washington, D.C., ghetto, and black viewers may identify with Ray's situation and his critique of the black criminal lifestyle. However, social accuracy and the discourse of black authenticity are ultimately two different things. Ultimately, one must consider the constitutive impact of the discourses of black authenticity if one is to understand *Slam*'s appeal to both mainstream and multiracial audiences.

"Dropping Truth": *Def Poetry*'s Marketing of Spoken Word to the Mainstream

It's imperative that these spoken word artists be catapulted to the mainstream and be recognized. Finally the marriage between (Hip-hop/Rap) and spoken word can begin the arduous task of reconciliation.

—Bruce George, former executive producer of *Russell Simmons Presents Def Poetry*, "DPJ Roots"

Rap has been raped by marketing. Spoken word is still pure. It is up to the poets to keep it that way.

—Flowmentalz, a poet featured on *Russell Simmons Presents Def Poetry*, interviewed by Chaka Ferguson

In 2002, cable television audiences got another chance to experience spoken word poetry on-screen, this time under the brand of HBO's series *Russell Simmons Presents Def Poetry*. Soon after the series debuted, poets from the show appeared at U.S. colleges and universities as part of a *Def Poetry* tour, reading their work in live performances with celebrity emcees such as Chuck D from the rap group Public Enemy. At the same time, other poets performed in a stage version of *Def Poetry* in San Francisco, a show that eventually made its way to New York City's Broadway circuit in November of 2002. The Peabody-award-winning cable series celebrated its sixth (and presumably last) season on HBO in 2007 and during its tenure was advertised as one of the network's hottest original series alongside such staples as *The Sopranos, Deadwood,* and *Six Feet Under.* As of summer 2008, no plans have been announced for the continuation of the series. Still, the popularity of *Def Poetry* on stage and screen during the first part of this decade would suggest that its poets—many of whom have performed at National Poetry Slams—have gained a mainstream following. This popularity also suggests to managers and broadcast executives that there was and may still be a viable market for spoken word poetry.

There are obvious connections between hip-hop and spoken word as genres; they are lyrical art forms with similar overall media histories. Before Russell Simmons's projects, however, they had vastly different commercial histories. In the 1990s, hip-hop was a multi-billion-dollar industry reaching all corners of the popular media, while spoken word poetry struggled to find a wider audience. The now defunct Mouth Almighty records, founded by Bob Holman (creator of the PBS series *The United States of Poetry*), was a recording venture for spoken word poetry that showed promise in the mid-1990s, but it failed to find a large market and eventually went under. Only in the last several years has spoken word poetry gained mainstream and commercial notoriety. This popularity has surfaced in the generic crossover between hip-hop and spoken word, a crossover promoted by hip-hop recording executives who stand to benefit by signing up-and-coming spoken word poets. It is as if the recording industry has lent hip-hop's commercial viability to spoken word poetry, a commercial crossover that promises artists who reflect hip-hop aesthetics will be the first to be shunted into the limelight. *Russell Simmons Presents Def Poetry* is the first example of the widespread commercial success of spoken word poetry, for, although films such as *Slam* and *Slamnation* did achieve a modicum of mainstream critical attention and sought mainstream audiences, they also circulated primarily in independent commercial venues.

Russell Simmons, figurehead of the *Def Poetry* productions, is a hip-hop recording mogul whose roster of accomplishments includes managing the rap group Run-DMC in the early 1980s, cofounding the Def Jam recording label in 1984, producing the HBO series *Def Comedy Jam* in 1991, and founding the Phat Farm hip-hop clothing line in 1992. His career has been characterized by marrying business interests with hip-hop culture; a 2003 *Business Week* cover story hailed Simmons with the title "The CEO of Hip-Hop."[40] Ever dedicated to the African American community, his business activities have recently been supplemented with political activism among black and urban youth. In 2001, partnering with the former executive director of the National Association for the Advancement of Colored People (NAACP), Benjamin F.

Chavis, Simmons founded the Hip-Hop Summit Action Network, an organization that sponsors voter initiatives, educational reform, and community programs targeting the hip-hop generation (which critic Bakari Kitwana identifies as African Americans born between 1965 and 1984).[41] Still, Simmons remains a shrewd entrepreneur and has succeeded in building an empire of businesses that center around, if not define and produce, hip-hop culture. These projects reflect his self-proclaimed goal of "the 'hip-hopification' of American media."[42]

Simmons's projects are known not only for promoting black artists to black audiences but also for attracting "crossover" white audiences; Run-DMC, for example, is generally recognized as the first rap group to attract such an audience and the first to be featured by mainstream media sources such as *Rolling Stone* magazine and MTV.[43] Similarly, *Def Comedy Jam* introduced white and black audiences alike to a new cadre of black comedians, including Bernie Mac, Cedric the Entertainer, Martin Lawrence, Steve Harvey, Chris Tucker, Jamie Foxx, and Chris Rock, by exercising the "for us, by us" philosophy. As much as these stand-up performances may have been intended for (and indeed taped in front of) predominately black audiences, it appears, as Samuels suggests of rap, that even the most racially exclusive forms of entertainment can be popular with white mainstream audiences in part *because* they are racially exclusive and lend Def Jam projects an air of insiderism (and hence authenticity). For these artists, as it has been for many black performers, going mainstream and earning a commercial presence has usually meant gaining an audience among young, white, middle-class consumers in addition to black consumers.

Simmons himself confirms this appeal to mainstream audiences; in an interview, he stated of spoken word poetry, "It's not edgy, fringe or even new. It's very mainstream; all stuff I get involved with is. . . . I don't think of commercial art in a negative way. I think of commercial art as art that speaks to a lot of people."[44] *Def Poetry* has approached this market share by contextualizing spoken word poetry within traditionally black hip-hop culture. Although the cable show features poets across the racial spectrum, the majority of its poets are African American, and many of its artists reflect hip-hop aesthetics in their work by employing rhythmically rhymed language, urban subject matter, and hip-hop slang. The show takes much of its on-screen flavor from its emcee, Mos Def, a famous rapper and actor from Brooklyn; the show itself is taped in New York City. Between acts, a DJ spins hip-hop tracks, and

Mos Def sometimes performs a call-and-response ritual at the beginning of the show ("Where Harlem at? Where Queens at? Brooklyn, stand up!"). The choice to have a readily recognizable hip-hop artist host the show is a deliberate gesture toward bringing hip-hop audiences to spoken word poetry, and Mos Def's occasional freestyle rapping further emphasizes a connection between the two. Simmons's perfunctory appearance at the end of each episode (in which he usually embraces Mos Def, states to the audience "I hope you were inspired. God Bless," and quickly exits) seals the connection between the hip-hop and poetry worlds and helps to lend the show commercial legitimacy. All of these elements work to cross racial boundaries and target the mainstream audience for hip-hop albums—a young audience that includes white, middle-class listeners—as the audience for spoken word poetry.

Furthermore, spoken word poetry's current association with hip-hop plays on a tension between artistic "purity" and commercialism in popular American culture. The two epigraphs that begin this section reflect that tension. Bruce George represents the marketer's point of view, suggesting that making a link between hip-hop and spoken word poetry is a positive step and will help the latter achieve mainstream commercial success. Flowmentalz, on the other hand, reflects the widespread opinion among spoken word poets that commercial attention will prove to be negative for the art form. He suggests that most hip-hop is created with commercial interests in mind while spoken word poetry remains untouched by such interests and is therefore a more authentic mode of lyrical expression. Both opinions, although they seem to directly compete with each other, are essential to spoken word poetry's commercial success. Indeed, it is precisely this tension that enhances the spoken word poet's current cachet with mainstream audiences. Displaying mastery of the rapper's idiom while critiquing the rapper's hackneyed and materialistic public image, the spoken word poet working in the hip-hop idiom lays claim not only to lyrical authenticity but to racial authenticity—a highly valuable commodity in today's mainstream youth markets. Under this highly stylized, politically conscious brand of verse, poetry has become cool.

To compound the show's crossover youth appeal, the HBO series features famous recording stars (such as Erykah Badu, George Clinton, Common, Jewel, the Last Poets, Smokey Robinson, and Kanye West), "icon" poets of literary note (such as Amiri Baraka, Nikki Giovanni, Joy Harjo, Linton Kwesi Johnson, Haki Madhubuti, Sharon Olds, Sonia

Sanchez, and Sekou Sundiata), and celebrities (such as Benjamin Bratt, Dave Chappelle, and Malcolm Jamal Warner) alongside the spoken word poets. As on the National Poetry Slam stage, many of the poets featured on the *Def Poetry* series are politically outspoken and perform work about their identities. Most of the poets featured are also from large urban areas such as New York, Atlanta, Chicago, and Los Angeles, and the subjects of poverty, crime, imprisonment, racism, and violence are commonly addressed. From the Twin Poets' recitation of their poem "Dreams Are Illegal in the Ghetto" to Keith Murray's poem in which he recounts being raised by a convict father, "Manchild," many poets appearing on the show attest to the trials and celebrations of black, urban, underclass experiences common to hip-hop music.

The series has also featured comedians from the *Def Comedy Jam* stage, including Jamie Foxx and Cedric the Entertainer, performing routines that parody other images of the black poet circulating in mainstream culture and that legitimate—if not authenticate—the "def" spoken word poet. Jamie Foxx performed a character sketch on the show dressed in Afrocentric garb and comically waving a stick of incense. He performed a poem entitled "Off the Hizzle for Shizzle" in which he has a one-night stand with a woman who steals his money and gives him a venereal disease. The performance is a rhymed parody of two common images of the spoken word artist in black culture: the Afrocentric poet and the rapper bragging about his latest sexual conquest. His dress and wild gesticulations with the incense reflect his critique of the former; his abundant use of "izzle" pig latin to rhyme reflects his parody of the latter.[45]

Cedric the Entertainer's performance is similarly critical of the Afrocentric poet's image. He describes a coffeehouse on "poetry night" where "African drums beat," and he finds poets embodying clichés such as "the dreadlock hair and Erykah Badu music, soulchild, headwrap-wearing brother that talks like *this* and gonna tell me way too much about his childhood, or how the white man keep keepin' tha brotha down, or use the word *molasses* in so many forms that I don't even wanna put syrup on my damn pancakes."[46] Then, shifting into semiregular rhyme, Cedric contrasts this "clichéd" work with that of the spoken word artists appearing on *Def Poetry,* poets who "send you on cerebral vacations and mind excavations" and demonstrate that "words are often the tools that separate us from the fools." He concludes by endorsing the poetry as it appears on the *Def Poetry* series:

"To the spoken word artist, I give you your props, your kudos, and your standing Os. 'Coz not only are you the hot butter with the toast, but you now have your own *jam*." Notably, Cedric employs rhyme only when delivering his encomium for the spoken word poet, formally marking the break from his comedic monologue to lyrical expression and his temporary shift from "def comic" to "def poet" on the HBO stage.

Cedric's and Foxx's performances illustrate that even though the HBO series places spoken word poetry within a highly commodified vision of black urban culture *Def Poetry* performances such as these can be, as Tricia Rose notes of hip-hop, "a public and highly accessible place where black meanings and perspectives—even as they are manipulated by corporate concerns—can be shared and validated among black people."[47] These meanings are, I would add, intimately connected to the intercultural and multiracial exchanges that take place in mainstream venues such as the *Def Poetry* series. Even if *Def Poetry* is intended for black audiences under the "for us, by us" philosophy, the commercial airwaves themselves do not discriminate in their viewership (except, of course, if one cannot afford the subscription fee for the cable network). In the entertainment industry, gaining a white, middle-class audience is synonymous with achieving mainstream success. When white audiences tune in to watch a show so focused on representing African American poets and culture, what happens? In these moments, which could be most accurately described as "cultural eavesdropping," the meaning of blackness itself is negotiated and exchanged between and across race and class spectrums.

As in many mainstream venues, poets have used the *Def Poetry* stage to critique hip-hop culture, offering an image of the spoken word poet as more virtuosic, and hence authentic, than the rapper. For example, in one episode the National Poetry Slam champion Sekou tha Misfit performs a parody of the now hackneyed rapper's braggadocio entitled "The Rapper." In the persona of a hard-core thug, he details the wealth, sexual conquests, and the adulating company that rap-star status affords his character while revealing the emptiness of each aspect of this lifestyle. Throughout the body of the poem, the rapper's rhetoric is revealed as false: though a high roller, he sheepishly admits to the audience, "I'm broke"; though a pimp, he admits, "I respect women"; though bragging about his use of semiautomatic weapons, he admits, "I don't own a gun." Speaking first in the rapper's voice and then in his own as a spoken word poet, Sekou concludes:

Of all ya'll hard thugs I'm the hardest
Leave your ass dearly departed, or severely retarded
. . . .
I'm hard—hard as the eyes of killer, hard as the hands of a slave,
I've never known love, and never been afraid,
I'm hard as a body that's dead, hard as a convict's bed,
Hard as my d—k when I'm getting head—**but the truth is. . .**
I'm scared . . .

(I'm scared.)

> **See, the emcee is the one who'll *whisper* the truth.**
> **The rapper is the one who'll *holla* the lies.**
> **So don't act surprised at what your daughter knows when**
> **she's five**
> **Just blame it on the bullsh-t that you buy—*look what***
> ***you've done . . .***

I'm a rapper.[48]

Overall, Sekou critiques the commercial artificialities of the rapper and champions the authenticity of the spoken word poet (here figured as the "emcee"). The performance of the poem complements its rhetorical structure, which figures the rapper as the consummate Iago. The rapper's criminal boasts are made in character, loudly and publicly, while his truthful admissions are made in confidential asides to his audience (indicated here by the author's use of smaller type)—"I'm broke," "I'm lonely," "I don't have a gun," "I respect women," and finally, "I'm scared." Sekou underscores this duplicity by whispering these asides, and he indicates in italics moments when the dynamics of volume come into play. In the final lines of the poem, he breaks out of character (as indicated in boldface), entering his "authentic" identity as a spoken word poet and asking the members of his audience to justify their consumption of gansta rap. Sekou's poem is an example of the critique and renegotiation of the representation of blackness in mainstream American culture and media, pointing to the political possibilities of commercial projects such as *Def Poetry*.

Still, one must not ignore the commercial interests of the series, those of Simmons's Def Jam and Phat Farm enterprises, the agents who represent these artists, and HBO. Even the title of the series reflects commercial branding. The initial conceptual person on the project, the self-described grassroots poet and former executive producer of *Def Poetry,* Bruce George, revealed in a 2002 interview that he wanted to call the program *Def Poetry Jam* from the start but he had yet to get permission from Simmons to use the Def Jam brand. He also considered the title *Def Poetry Slam,* but he ran into a "quagmire" with Poetry Slam, Incorporated, the nonprofit organization that stages the annual National Poetry Slam, whose constituents had concerns about the commercial nature of the program. George admitted that he "wanted to go with 'jam' to keep the branding that *Def Comedy Jam* had. I wanted to establish a feed off of that branding. And that's one of the reasons why *Def Poetry* is doing so well, is because of the fact that it's feeding off the branding of *Def Comedy Jam,* it's feeding off the branding of the record label Def Jam." George compared the mainstream commercialization of poetry to that of rap. Rap music, he posited, in its shift from an art form of unity to one of gangstaism, "went from consciousness to consumption." Spoken word poetry, he predicted, would probably experience the same growing pains during its period of "bastardization" in mainstream culture.

> Since poetry is moving from the sidestream to the mainstream, there are a lot of people in the music industry that want to jump on the bandwagon and follow Russell's lead. . . . So the big picture is gaining penetration in the record industry, . . . in VHS and DVD markets, . . . more national tours, more national competitions, major sponsors like Verizon and AT&T. . . . The big picture is it being a lot more commercial.[49]

Indeed, during the life of the series, *Def Poetry* became a highly visible part of the Def Jam media franchise; one can now buy DVDs of all six of the HBO series' seasons and an anthology of work by performers in the Broadway show. Some of the poets on the series wear Phat Farm fashions, and both Mos Def and Russell Simmons almost always appear in Phat Farm gear. In a performance tradition in which truth, authenticity, and realness are at a premium (as Sekou tha Misfit's poem underscores), it is easy to forget the commercial forces behind how poets appear on the program as well as who is selected to perform. The program uses celebrity performers to attract popular audiences and well-established poets writing predominately out of the Black Arts tradition to give spoken word poetry a legitimate literary and ethnic history. The young, multiracial studio audience seems enthusiastic about these performances, bopping their heads to hip-hop music and applauding intermittently at the delivery of strong liberal political messages. This hip, young, alternative, and diverse studio audience is part of *Def Poetry's* constructed environment and easily obscures the commercial interests of the show and Simmons's investment in bringing spoken word poetry to the mainstream.

Yet another example of Def Jam's marketing of spoken word to mainstream audiences is *Def Poetry Jam on Broadway,* the stage show that ran for nearly six months on the Great White Way and garnered a 2003 Tony for Best Special Theatrical Event.[50] Produced by Russell Simmons and directed by Stan Lathan (who also counts the HBO *Def Poetry* series, *The Bernie Mac Show, Moesha, Martin,* and *Cedric "the Entertainer" Presents* among his directing credits), the two-hour show featured nine spoken word poets, the majority of whom have experience on the National Poetry Slam stage.

Advertised as "Voices of the Next America," the cast's racial and ethnic diversity and urban background are consistently noted by both promoters and theater reviewers. The poets include Beau Sia, a Chinese American raised in Oklahoma and a resident of Los Angeles; Black Ice (Lamar Manson), an African American poet from North Philadelphia; Staceyann Chin, a queer Jamaican national from New York City; Steve Colman, a Caucasian from New York City; Mayda del Valle, a Boriqua poet raised on Chicago's South Side; Georgia Me (Tamika Harper), an African American woman from Atlanta; Suheir Hammad, a Brooklyn-born Palestinian American woman; Lemon, a Brooklyn b-boy of Puerto Rican descent; and Poetri, a middle-class African American male from Los Angeles. Sia, Chin, Colman, del Valle, and Poetri all have experience as National Poetry Slam champions. Rounding out the cast is DJ Tendaji (Tendaji Lathan, the director's son), who pumps up the audience before the show by mixing old-school funk and hip-hop tunes on his turntable.[51]

The Broadway show's set, designed by Bruce Ryan, reflects it urban emphasis. The stage is relatively bare with seven uneven doorframes and steps set at canted angles painted in grays and beiges; together they abstractly suggest brownstone stoops. There is a table for the disc jockey, who is onstage spinning hip-hop music between performances, to one side of the stage. Behind the door frames, instead of a velvet curtain or backdrop, the brick wall of the Longacre Theater looms. Although the theater scholar Jill Dolan describes the set as lacking specificity, the textures of metal and brick in the context of the show suggest an abstract city landscape, an urban chic.[52] It is clear that this is no production of *Our Town*. This urban sensibility is also reflected in the cast's costuming, which was designed by Paul Tazewell; with the exception a few of the women (most notably the diva Georgia Me, who is costumed in custom leather outfits and fly designer sunglasses), most of the poets take the stage in hip-hop jerseys, tank tops, baseball caps, baggy jeans, tennis shoes, and thrift store finds.[53]

The show itself features forty-one poems of about two to five minutes in length. All poems, including the handful of ensemble pieces performed in the production, are original compositions performed by their authors, just as at a slam. The entire program is roughly organized around themes of identity and culture, heroes and heroines, love, and nationality. The final poem, "I Write America," is performed by the entire cast and is an opportunity for the poets to reflect on what being American means to them. Both critical and optimistic of how America regards difference, they reflect on various aspects of their race, class, and sexual identities, a diversity they emphasize by talking over each other at the close of the show to create a verbal dissonance.

As this final poem reflects, members of the *Def Poetry Jam* cast repeatedly, and many times angrily, comment on issues of identity. The confrontational tone of much of this work has not escaped notice. Writing in the neoconservative periodical *Commentary*, John McWhorter says of the Broadway performance, "[T]heir reigning theme [was] a contemptuous indictment of the American status quo. *Def Poetry Jam* was, in fact, less a show than a rally. Facing front, proudly smug, the performers were saying that either you were with them or you were a clueless bigot."[54] The "hollering" and "shouting" McWhorter notes of many of the poet-performers may indeed serve a divisive purpose, one consistent with many performance poetry movements discussed in this book: the performance of a "renegade" identity that opposes the academy and dominant culture. McWhorter's characterization of the show as a rally is quite accurate in this respect, as poets (and often audiences) seek to consider spoken word performance as a social, as well as literary, movement. Dolan considers the show "a public sphere in which social relations might be rehearsed" between poets and audiences.[55]

Despite Simmons's assertion that the diversity of the *Def Poetry Jam on Broadway* cast was a coincidence, the show's marketing team and director have played up the urban and multicultural identities of the cast. This vision of "the Next America"—of the cultural hybridity and difference that can blossom in urban centers such as New York—is perhaps the most prominent theme tying the show together. The poets' racial and class differences, as well as their critique of the "melting pot" ideology, are also the most common elements reviewers note. Phillip Hopkins writes, "Not only is this incredibly diverse group just as American as the whiter-toned casts more familiar to Broadway audiences, the impression is that they have thought deeply about what the idea of America means because their own experiences are so often at odds with this country's promises."[56] For other reviewers, this theme rang false. "In general," Martin Denton notes, "none of us would dispute the show's main themes—poverty *does* beget violence; powerful institutions *do* ignore the problems of the underprivileged; minority groups *are* discriminated against in America. But neither would any of us be startled by any of these ideas—there's very little original or interesting thinking in evidence here."[57]

It seems that for better or worse the *Def Poetry Jam on Broadway* hopes to promote and capitalize on the "hipness" of the voices of people of color proclaiming their identities against the status quo. The discourses of marginality abundantly present in the show are discourses that hip-hop and spoken word poetry share to different degrees. They also share claims to authenticity, truth, and realness; for example, the *San Francisco Chronicle* printed a review of the stage show entitled, "Uplifting Hip-Hop Show Really Tells It Like It Is: Well-Versed Poets are Funny and Earthy in 'Def Poetry Jam.'"[58] This cloying discourse of authenticity does not exist solely in the opinion of the reviewers; just as in slam poetry, performers and organizers promote *Def Poetry Jam* as "the real deal." Director Stan Lathan remarks, "There are so many shows I've seen, not just in theater but even more in television, that start out with the hook 'This is telling it like it is. . . . But in the translation from the original concept to the stage or screen it gets diluted. With the poets, my philosophy is, 'Let's put it up there, let's find the best people to perform it and let's get out of their way.'"[59] Lathan's comments suggest that this hands-off approach is taken to allow the poets to "tell it like it is" or at least tell it like they see it. Black Ice says with near evangelical fervor that he prefers the noncompetitive format of *Def Poetry Jam* to the openly competitive environment of poetry slams because "my mission in this lifetime is to spread the truth. And when we have a competition of truth, it makes no sense that my truth is truer than yours. Truth can't be conquered, it can only be built upon. And we're dropping truth."[60]

And yet both *Def Poetry Jam*'s promotional materials and Black Ice's own work directly suggest that the truth of his experience is precisely in competition with the rapper's. As further proof of this discourse of authenticity, consider this excerpt from the biography of Black Ice that appears in the *Def Poetry Jam on Broadway* companion anthology.

> The Philadelphia streets grew his potent poetry. Lamar didn't grow up soft. . . . He was a local shining star, both as a hustler and a fledgling hip-hopper. "I grew up slinging coke and rapping, but finally, I settled down and became a barber and coke dealer. I was still a barber up until a year ago. . . . When I decided to leave the street game my words and my life began to flourish."
>
> Broadway was a hard routine for an ex-hustler to crack, but "Ice" never missed a show; a testimony to how much he's turned himself into the messenger of the earth he was destined to be. "Every night I had to re-invent those poems because there is someone out in that audience that needs to hear what I'm about to spit."
>
> . . . While Black Ice has elevated himself above a street hustler, he did not abandoned [*sic*] the streets for the lights of Broadway. He's still keeping it real.[61]

This biography, presumably written by the anthology's editor, Danny Simmons, reflects many aspects of the typical commercial rhetoric surrounding black spoken word artists. Most prominently featured are Black Ice's street credentials, conveyed by emphasizing his rough-and-tumble urban youth, his status as a drug dealer, his skills as a hip-hop emcee, and his working-class career as a barber. His "talent and love for art," the narrative argues, was a rehabilitating force that saved him from his dangerous criminal lifestyle. Thus, although Black Ice has "elevated himself above a street hustler," the biographical-cum-promotional text assures readers that he still very much retains the authenticity of the street. Here, as in several other commercial representations of spoken word poetry, the black male artist is the gangsta reformed through poetic expression.

Black Ice's own poetry attests to this reformation. In "Front Page," for example, he repeatedly contrasts his "honest," "loyal," and "righteous" path with the artificial boasts of the gangsta rapper, whom he calls "just another / Motherfucking nigga."

> How the fuck you figure your shit is bigger
> Than mine
> I see you diamond blinking
> Cuban Linking and full length minking
> All strung out on disillusional thinking
>
> . . . .
>
> You continue to hide your true self
> Behind gangsta' movie disguises
> Oblivious to what life's true prize is
> Equating stupidity with the length you
> Think your dick size is[62]

In another poem performed both in the Broadway production and on the HBO series, "410 Days in the Life," Black Ice explicitly refutes the materialistic and violent image of the rapper with a record deal, making his own claim to authenticity as a spoken word poet.

> Nigga I give a fuck how
> slick you flowin'
> if you ain't showin' nothin'
> to these kids
> or
> adding nothing positive
> to the Earth . . .
> Black Ice been destined
> to touch the world ever since
> I was born,
> to be real,
> fuck a record deal . . .
> God
> Gives me what I'm worth.[63]

It is important to note here that Black Ice, like a handful of other spoken word poets who appear in the *Def Poetry* projects, frequently acknowledges his religious faith. In this respect, his image as a spoken word poet takes on another aspect: he has been spiritually as well as socially reformed through his practice of verse.

Black Ice isn't the only member of the cast to address the image of the urban black underclass male onstage. Georgia Me performs a poem entitled "Nig-gods" in which she proclaims her attraction to black men who are "ghetto superstars" and "fly as fuck" but who also "seek knowledge" and are "conscious of the true plan."[64] In this, she supports the socially conscious image of the spoken word poet offered by *Def Poetry Jam*. Other members of the cast also perform aspects of marginalized racial, gender, and sexual identities onstage. Lemon and Mayda del Valle perform a duet about Tito Puente and their urban Boriqua backgrounds, Poetri and Georgia Me perform comedic pieces about growing up overweight in the black community, Suheir Hammad performs a poem about being profiled in line at airport security because of her Palestinian American heritage, and Staceyann Chin performs several poems about her lesbian and Jamaican identities. In this respect, the only white member of the cast, Steve Colman, appears to be the odd man out. His performances are largely about subjects beyond himself and his identity; his poetry lingers on themes of government corruption and the transformative power of poetry itself (e.g., "I wanna hear a poem / where ideas kiss similes so deeply / metaphors get jealous").[65]

Since the first whispers about the *Def Poetry* projects, poets in the slam community have weighed the benefits of reaching a larger mainstream audience against the negative associations conjured by going commercial; for the majority of these poets, the former outweighs the latter. Colman and del Valle, for instance, "are happy to see their brand of spoken word performance in its 'commercial infancy,' despite the fact that some might consider them sellouts. (The art form is similar to rap in its early days, they say)."[66] Similarly, Simmons makes no apologies for his or his performers' commercial intentions, insisting that def poets are "honest as the day is long" and retain their authenticity in his commercial ventures.[67] Spoken word poetry, he remarks in another interview, "is evolving to where it is very commercial. So it's just the natural growth of the movement that merited a vehicle."[68]

Both the *Def Poetry* television series and the *Def Poetry Jam* stage show commercially target young audiences, especially the hip-hop generation of twenty- and thirty-somethings that comprise their casts.[69] Although the series' studio audiences are always quite racially diverse and primarily black, the HBO series is likely to encounter more white, middle-class viewers at home. At the performance of *Def Poetry Jam on Broadway* that I attended, the audience appeared to be racially diverse; roughly half was white, certainly much more diverse than the average Broadway audience, which tends to be overwhelmingly white. It was also remarkably young; the vast majority of audience members appeared to be under thirty, another rarity for a Broadway audience. Such observations indicate that the live performance staged in an urban center such as New York City has the potential to attract a more diverse audience than the HBO show does in American living rooms. The price of a ticket may also be a deciding factor in attracting an audience of varying incomes; tickets ranged anywhere from twenty-five to sixty-five dollars, which ranks as a very reasonable price for a Broadway show. Those in the cheaper mezzanine seats were notably younger than those seated on the orchestra level, yet another indication that Simmons's marketing team is making significant headway in targeting a youth market.

The youth of the *Def Poetry Jam* audience is probably a reflection of the market crossover of hip-hop and spoken word, as hip-hop appeals to younger audiences. It is also a reflection of the subject matter and tone of the performances onstage. An enchanted *New York Times* reviewer notes, "For all the didacticism in "Def Poetry," there's a thrill in seeing young people actually work up steam about the sorry state of the world. . . . How nice to smell springtime in the land of mothballs."[70]

The Politics of Selling Out: Some Pros and Cons

stealing me
was the smartest thing you ever did
too bad you don't teach the truth to your kids
my influence on you is the reflection you see
when you look into your minstrel mirror
and talk about your culture
  —Saul Williams, "Amethyst Rocks"

The political meanings of spoken word poetry's mainstream commercial success are varied and complex, to which the history of black popular music will attest. For artists of color, "selling out" usually entails the additional complexities of racial politics, for going mainstream means gaining a white following.[71] The common critique of these artists is that they have abandoned their racial communities in favor of white audiences and patrons. However accurate such critiques may be, selling out can also be a way for artists to disseminate subversive messages to mainstream audiences as well as an opportunity to discuss the meanings of racial identity on a national, if not global, stage. So the politics of spoken word poetry's introduction to mainstream commercial culture involve both sacrifice and possibility. The *Def Poetry Jam on Broadway* cast member Staceyann Chin says of her participation in the project, "The dance of survival in this new world of art and money is the dance of the middle ground—one has to straddle the commercial/mainstream and the not-for-profit/underground. . . . I am walking a tightrope between poetic prostitution and art—and that, my dear, is the only way not to die as an artist."[72]

In the case of black performers, white, middle-class audiences may reflect the illusion of black urban essence and authenticity by rewarding and consuming black performers' use of certain gestures, sounds, language patterns, rhythms, and topics, thereby reflecting a racialized desire. The slam community's well-meaning appreciation of marginalized identity is one such example of this desire, whether its ends are to distinguish slam poetry from a predominately white academic tradition or a way for white audience members to create liberal identities for themselves in public. This authenticity, as it is ascribed to black voices and narratives in the commercial sphere, can also signal the commodification of these voices. The scholar Amy Robinson notes that "exchanged . . . between proprietors and possessors of any and every ilk, marginal peoples take on the characteristics of commodity whose value is only relative to that of another."[73] The slam poet and activist Alix Olson encountered such an experience during the taping of an MTV poetry show pilot.

> Although the four performers are our peers, representing an assortment of ethnicities, races, and sexualities, the audience is a monolith of white, heterosexual couples. We learn later that models were invited to play audience members. "People at home want to relate to the audience," I am told.[74]

Olson's experience puts into relief acute troubles surrounding the popular media's reproduction, commodification, and consumption of spoken word poetry as it tries to reach mainstream audiences. Gareth Griffiths argues that "authentic speech, where it is conceived not as political strategy but as a fetishized cultural commodity, may be employed . . . to enact a discourse of 'liberal violence,' re-enacting its own oppressions on the subjects it purports to represent and defend."[75] Olson's MTV audience seems to exhibit this type of "liberal violence," and it is not the only entity to do so. Recognizing what rap did for Tommy Hilfiger products, Perry Ellis International presented black poets appearing in the movie *Slam* "Breakthrough awards" in the hope of making a marketing link between their products and spoken word poetry.[76] The "extreme" energy drink Red Bull has sponsored national Word Clash "street poetry" competitions in an attempt to access spoken word's young audience base in the United States. McDonald's recently jumped on the spoken word bandwagon with an advertising campaign featuring an African American woman waxing poetic about salads in what the company's director of marketing described as the "def poetry" mode.[77] Surveying the range of spoken word poetry video and audio recordings that are not self-produced and strive to find mainstream audiences, one will find that most performers are of color and the majority are African American. This trend seems to indicate that, like some brands of hip-hop, commercial interests in performance poetry are not wholly invested in promoting poetry itself but are instead invested in capitalizing on the perceived authenticity of black, urban, underclass expression and its popularity with the mainstream youth market.

The politics of the *Def Poetry* and *Slam* projects are nuanced and complex as they engage serious issues about race, reception, and representation in mainstream American culture. Just as with other performance poetry movements or black popular musical genres that went mainstream, there are benefits and disadvantages to a poet's entry into the commercial venue of spoken word poetry. The most obvious advantages are the profits and exposure that poets stand to receive by entering the mainstream arena. As a result of the *Def Poetry* Broadway show and the HBO series, it is more possible than ever for performance poets to make a living performing and recording their work full time, although only a handful actually do. Furthermore, the widespread dissemination of spoken word poetry via commercial media presents poets with a unique opportunity to influence a large, mainstream audience with diverse and subversive messages. Still, in order to do so poets must participate in a commercial system that may counteract those messages. Tricia Rose remarks of this paradigm in hip-hop:

To refuse to participate in the manipulative process of gaining access to video, recording materials, and performing venues is to almost guarantee a negligible audience and marginal cultural impact. To participate in and try to manipulate the terms of mass-mediated culture is a double-edged sword that cuts both ways—it provides communication channels within and among largely disparate groups and requires compromise that often affirms the very structures much of rap's philosophy seems determined to undermine.[78]

Such is the current conundrum of socially conscious spoken word poets regardless of race. For African American poets, the *Def Poetry* projects provide a forum for a new generation of empowering black meanings and aesthetics. Still, when marketers characterize or audiences perceive spoken word poetry as an authentic racial expression, it becomes clear that black urbanity has become a fetishized commodity in this genre as in hip-hop music (as the McDonald's commercial written in the "def poetry mode" exemplifies).

The commercial and political success of projects such as the *Def Poetry Jam* and the film *Slam* greatly relies on the tension between dominant and marginalized cultures, on the intersections and competing interests of the two. What makes spoken word poetry such a phenomenon is that it is commercially oriented yet politically subversive; while it may at times promote corporate interests, it also usually entails spreading a political message or sense of cultural awareness. In addition, while its language is sometimes homogeneous in style, space exists for that style to be parodied and sometimes radically reinvented (as Foxx and Cedric the Entertainer exemplify in their *Def Poetry* sketches). Thus, the commercial entity of spoken word poetry is representative of neither mainstream nor marginalized culture but is dependent on the tug-of-war between them. Like hip-hop, it is a genre that "is at once part of the dominant text and, yet, always on the margins of this text; relying on and commenting on the text's center and always aware of its proximity to the border."[79]

As the *Def Poetry* projects clearly privilege black artists and hip-hop aesthetics, what should we make of white poets in the spoken word arena? One reviewer pointedly states the case of the Broadway show's "lone white performer" writing in the rhymed and metered idiom of hip-hop: "Colman seems so blissfully unaware that, in appropriating the hip-hop vernacular and form from its originators, he is as much an exploitative white colonialist as the powerful people that he says he despises."[80] In a market where white rappers such as Eminem have been commercially successful, many artists and critics are rightly sensitive about this issue.

Still, the performances of many white poets who take on hip-hop aesthetics seem too nuanced to write off as simply appropriative; if they were merely that, their audiences would run them out on a rail. Instead, these performances seem more a testament to the kind of intercultural and interracial exchange that youth culture has always embraced. Just as the traditionally black art forms of soul, gospel, and R & B attracted crossover audiences and led to the social and cultural hybridity of black and white youth, spoken word poetry's crossover into the mainstream may serve as a new site for interracial exchange and possibility. As one critic notes of Simmons's projects:

> Nobody will be particularly convinced that a group of Beverly Hills kids adopting the gangsta lifestyle in terms of talk and dress will be anything but an unwitting parody. Yet, if the kids are looking at the same issues, they may eventually gather some empathy with those who are living the style for real. . . . And [def] poetry has simply taken the movement a few steps further.[81]

The mass consumption of spoken word poetry as a predominately black art form by white, liberal, middle-class audiences, however, still raises a much more urgent concern. If black poets are consumed as representing an authentic black experience, or are deemed "hip" simply because of their marginalized status, then the commercialization of performance poetry stands to further separate these poets from their mainstream audiences not bring them together. As in hip-hop, the consumption of spoken word through CDs, DVDs, television, and film rather than the reception of spoken word via live performance further worries the point because these products obliterate real contact between artists and their audiences. In this respect, the avid consumption of spoken word poets of color by white audiences can become a site of what Samuels calls "racial voyeurism" not racial exchange.[82] Thus, although white audiences may feel that, as Henry Louis Gates Jr. puts it, "by buying records they have made some kind of valid social commitment," they can actually do such artists a disservice.[83] It is the unthinking consumer, paired with a potentially uncaring corporate entity, who troubles me here. As in *Slam,* poets' discourses of marginality, of the "street," of race and class oppression might very well be the hottest thing because of their difference from the center, from the suburb, from race and class privilege. Because of the ambivalent politics involved in this dynamic and because of the invisibility of these politics to the unthinking consumer, this fetishistic pattern of consumption can afford marginalized people a mainstream audience while simultaneously marginalizing them *further.*

In the end, the issues raised by performances of blackness in commercial arenas are not unlike those of over 150 years ago in minstrel venues, although the patronage of spoken word poetry and blackface minstrelsy have obvious differences. In discussing the commodification of black expression, Eric Lott emphasizes that performances of blackness are performative: they are "a cultural invention, not some precious essence installed in black bodies."[84] The songs, dances, characters, and poetics of blackface performance, he notes, were often created by both black folk and whites together in an odd fieldwork of caricature with the white spectator in mind. Thus, the issue of authenticity is directly implicated in minstrelsy's commodification; whites paid to see a blackness that was simultaneously lauded for its authentic representation of slave folk and critiqued for its counterfeit nature as a performance enacted through the burnt cork mask.

Lott's articulation of minstrelsy's ambivalent desire for what is authentically black and at the same time counterfeit is, I believe, a valuable contribution toward understanding black performance in general. As in blackface minstrelsy, today's mainstream audiences for spoken word poetry exercise the conflicting and complex dynamics of desire for racial authenticity through their consumption of the genre. Perhaps this is the final appeal of spoken word poetry today; through poets' performances of identity, audiences are given the ultimate power to decide which expressions are authentic and which are counterfeit. In this sense, the desire exercised between poets and audiences in the commercial arena of spoken word is a play for cultural power and meaning, one that will continue to influence and be influenced by the racial landscape of U.S. verse and culture.

Epilogue

"Designs for Living"—Notes on the Future of Slam Poetry

It is time for the relative critical silence about slam poetry to be broken. In its life in the public sphere, both as a grassroots practice in local slams and as a larger commercial practice in the genre of spoken word poetry, slam poetry exhibits many of the qualities of other performance poetry movements in America. These include resistance to dominant culture and the academy, an emphasis on difference and marginalized identity, and a commitment to intercultural exchange. The growing history and influence of the poetry slam suggests that the practice is not just a passing fad. The slam has brought new, young audiences to American poetry using unorthodox methods, a blend of different media, and a method of competitive, public critique. A practice now over twenty years old, the poetry slam brings to light incredibly complex issues of identity and performance in American culture, and its impact on poets from across the spectrum—academic, popular, and avant-garde—begs for slam poetry to be seriously considered among other popular poetry movements of the twentieth and twenty-first centuries. Yet it is still rare to find critical material on slam poetry that is more substantive than a case study or review.

This lack of serious scholarly attention did not occur because academic scholars have written off slam poetry altogether or, on the other hand, are just not hip enough to understand its appeal. It is because such poetry demands of its critic a new, interdisciplinary language that takes into account the complex set of literary, performance, and cultural issues that such work brings to the fore. To understand the full appeal of slam poetry and its claims to authenticity, one must go beyond traditional literary concerns and discuss the cultural politics of difference in America. After all, what makes poets such as Patricia Smith and Saul Williams remarkable cannot be measured merely by their use of narrative, meter, rhyme, or other oral acrobatics. The serious critic must cease treating the slam as a literary novelty or oddity and recognize it for what it is: a movement that combines (and at times exploits) the literary, performative, and social potential of verse and does so with the popular audience as its judge and guide.

As this body of criticism begins to emerge, the slam's audiences and practitioners will wonder: What is the future of slam poetry? What will happen as its artists migrate across the boundaries of taste and culture? Will slam poetry's serious consideration in the academy signal its demise as a populist phenomenon? Over time, slam poetry may indeed, like Beat or Black Arts poetry, become assimilated into the academy or dominant culture. But I believe this synthesis will be less an appropriation of slam poetry than an assertion of its influence. In blending poetry, performance, and politics, slam's influence is more pervasive than a bevy of small gatherings held in bars and coffee shops across America. On a national level, it has nurtured a new generation of poets who fuse poetry, musicality, and performance in varied and exciting ways. Poets such as Tyehimba Jess, Jeffrey McDaniel, and Regie Gibson, who have both MFAs and slam accolades, are becoming more common, and their writing proves that there is great potential in applying the tools of craft from both worlds. Their work also strongly refutes the criticism that the poetry performed at slams consists of all politics and no craft.

The term *crossover poet*—a poet who can succeed on both the page and the stage or one who operates in both academic and slam venues—is really a misnomer, for it makes these poets sound like anomalies rather than what they really are: poets who are redefining the American lyric through a fusion of media, politics, and aesthetics. Like R & B musicians who broke the racial barriers between white and black audiences and brought a new sound into American popular culture, these poets trouble the existing lines between poetry's elite and popular audiences, text and performance, form and free verse. Expanding poetry's audience has for too long been synonymous with expanding its readership, and the work of these artists argues for a paradigm shift in what we understand contemporary poetry to be and do. The story that is the future of slam and spoken word poetry is, I believe, part of the much larger story of American poetry as verse makes its way from subculture to dominant culture, from small printed volumes to prime-time television, and to all the hybrid places in between.

Such a change in the critical understanding of performance poetry's reach and influence will not take place without difficulty. It will be strange, and it will be contentious. America has already heard the claims that slam poetry is not real poetry or is just plain bad poetry, and yet audiences for such work continue to grow in both the public and commercial spheres. Rather than dismissing the tastes of these audiences (for an audience that fills seats for any kind of poetry on a Friday night is not one whose intelligence we should insult), I believe there is something more important going on at poetry slams than mere poetic versions of *American Idol*. In a literary culture where putting a poem into performance has, for the most part, meant an author imparting text aloud into the air, slam poetry challenges the dominant paradigm of poetry as a singular, private engagement between text and reader. Instead, it suggests that poetry is something performatively exchanged between poets and audiences in public and across several kinds of media, with all of the attending social and political contexts that enter into that cultural exchange. The idea that poetry is not just about aesthetic enjoyment but about constructing the identities of poets and audiences, performing social relationships, and establishing public communities of critics is profound. In the September 2006 issue of *Poetry,* John Barr, president of the richest poetry organization in the country, the Poetry Foundation, declared that there was nothing "new" going in contemporary poetry.[1] Clearly, he wasn't looking in the right place. This critical blindness to what is so apparently visible to popular audiences is a clarion signal that more traditional, established understandings of what poetry is and does must shift.

Slam poetry is work that has the potential to be both formative and transformative. Slams are not merely literary exercises or entertaining performances but events in which individuals have the potential to influence audiences and reify, change, or otherwise trouble positions of identity. They are what the anthropologist Martin Singer would call "cultural performances," performances that reflect and affect cultural values and expressions of the self in society. The anthropologist Victor Turner adds that "cultural performances are not simple reflectors or expressions of culture or even of changing culture but may themselves be active agencies of change, representing the eye by which culture sees itself and the drawing board on which creative actors sketch out what they believe to be more apt or interesting 'designs for living.'"[2]

As venues of cultural performance where status and identity can be expressed, debated, evaluated, and reconfigured, slams can be culturally transformative events for both poets and audiences. In performing their own "designs for living," slam poets may, in whatever small way, change the way audiences view and experience identity politics. In this respect, poetry slams can be sites of political congress and cultural contest. Poetry slams are places where, as the poet Ron Silliman argues, "simple everyday stylizations of the word take on new qualities of social resistance."[3]

This last impulse is the reason why Miguel Algarín, a former Rutgers University professor and cofounder of the Nuyorican Poets Café, dubbed the practice of poetry slams "the democratization of verse." As an open venue, the poetry slam is continually welcoming new audiences and practitioners into its ranks, all of whom can have a say in what is rewarded at the slam and where the art form is going. Poetry slams create communities of poets and poetry lovers in which verse is not only disseminated but discussed, critiqued, debated, and even reinvented. Such a democratic, critical strain is woefully absent from so many other public poetry projects designed in the wake of the "Can Poetry Matter?" years, projects that focus on getting poetry out to readers for consumption and enjoyment but don't invite its discussion or vital sense of community.

My own involvement in local and national poetry slams over the last dozen years demands that I highlight one thing that makes this group of artists so remarkable. Although the tenor of slam competition is sometimes cutthroat (trash talk and strategy sessions abound at slams when the stakes are high), the poetry slam is at its heart a place meant to celebrate its community and nurture new writers and performers regardless of their credentials. For some poets, the slam provides a place of acceptance where they otherwise could find none, and so it should come as no surprise that the slam boasts of a much more diverse group of poets—both in demographics and in style—than one will find in more elite circles. The slam's openness has ushered in a new awareness of and enthusiasm for the oral and performative possibilities of poetry among popular audiences. But beyond that, the poetry slam has also encouraged the formation of critical communities around poetry, figuring its audience as more than consumers. This may not be the manifestation of Whitman's "great audience" or necessarily the stuff of "Great Authors," but it certainly is a community with a great potential to shape American literary culture in the years to come.

Still, the poetry slam is far from a verse utopia. Slam poets, even though they are told by emcees to check their egos at the door, sometimes don't. And, let's face it, the competitive aspect of slam can bring out the worst in people. Nor is the poetry slam a one-stop panacea for poetry's once ailing life in the public sphere. If poetry is to become a part of a general audience's life, it must do so in variety and abundance on both the page and the stage and in all the media in between.

The poetry slam has been incredibly successful at creating one thing that other contemporary public poetry projects have not: a close-knit, distinct, and vibrant community of writers and patrons. We refer to our clan as the "slam family," dysfunction and all. As someone who identifies as an academic poet, a slam poet, and a critic, and as someone who is active in all of those arenas, I must say that I have not found a community as welcoming and permanent as this one. Even though most of us retire from competition at some point, a good number of slammers move on to have another, larger relationship with poetry or performance whether as organizers of slam events, as actors or musicians, or as respected authors or teachers. Some of us have met husbands, wives, or life partners at a slam. Many of us have met lifelong friends. We convene at our national competitions to revel in the possibilities of poetry in performance, geek out on our latest reading, debate what's new in spoken word poetry, and boogie. It's a great party. In such matters, the words of slammaster Allan Wolf—"The points are not the point, the point is poetry"—ring true.

The interdisciplinary nature of this book is my attempt to begin a serious critical conversation about slam poetry, spoken word poetry, and their attendant cultural and political complexities. In some respects, however, the reach of slam poetry is best understood when experienced in the intimate context of live performance. If you go to a slam and stick around long enough, you'll probably hear a poem you like. Or a poem you despise. Or a poem that changes your mind or your underwear. You decide. Because, *hey, you can do that at a slam.*

APPENDIX

DOCUMENT 1

The Official Rules of National Poetry Slam Competition

The Rules of the Slam

(At least, those we can agree on)

PSI gratefully acknowledges our "Guru of the Gray Area," Taylor Mali, the primary author of (and some say, impetus for) these rules, as well as the SlamMasters' Council who developed and adopted them.

"I have to submit to much in order to pacify the touchy
tribe of poets."

—Horace, 14 B.C.

These rules have been revised and tweaked at every SlamMasters' meeting since the first Chicago National Poetry Slam in 1991. Some debates have been ongoing for more than a decade. Loopholes have continually been closed, and many gray areas have been made either black or white. In the process, new loopholes and gray areas were probably created. But the rulebook was never intended to put an end to the healthy controversy that has always been an integral part of the slam. It will always be an attempt to agree on the wording (if not the spirit) of the rules of the National Poetry Slam as well as the consequences and penalties for breaking those rules. All we can hope for is to make the playing field as level as our trust in one another will allow.

These rules, along with the NPS Code of Honour, constitute a body of standards by which we agree to engage each other in this wacky thing we call Poetry Slam.

I. POEMS & PERFORMANCE

1) Poems can be on any subject and in any style.
2) Each poet must perform work that s/he has created.
3) No props.

From *The Official 2007 Poetry Slam Rulebook*

Generally, poets are allowed to use their given environment and the accoutrements it offers—microphones, mic stands, the stage itself, chairs on stage, a table or bar top, the aisle—as long as these accoutrements are available to other competitors as well. The rule concerning props is not intended to squelch the spontaneity, unpredictability, or on-the-fly choreography that people love about the slam; its intent is to keep the focus on the words rather than objects. Refer to Section V (Definitions) for further clarification on what is and is not a prop. Teams or individuals who inadvertently use a prop (for example, a timely yet unwitting grab at a necklace) can be immediately penalized two points if the emcee of the bout deems the effect of the violation to have been appreciable, but sufficiently lacking in specific intent. A formal protest need not be lodged before the emcee can penalize a poet or team in this way; however, the decision of the emcee can be appealed after the bout. Teams or individuals whose use of props in a poem appears to be more calculating and the result of a specific intent to enhance, illustrate, underscore, or otherwise augment the words of the poem will be given a retroactive score for the poem equal to two points less than the lowest scoring poem in that bout. This deduction, which can only be applied after a formal protest has been lodged against the offending team, will not be made by the emcee, but by a special committee assembled for this purpose.

4) No musical instruments or pre-recorded music.
5) No costumes. The protest committee may apply a two point deduction for violation of the costume rule.

Sampling

It is acceptable for a poet to incorporate, imitate, or otherwise "signify on" the words, lyrics, or tune of someone else (commonly called "sampling") in his own work. If he is only riffing off another's words, he should expect only healthy controversy; if on the other hand, he is ripping off their words, he should expect scornful contumely.

The No Repeat Rule

A poem may be only used once during the entire tournament.

The Three-Minute Rule

No performance should last longer than three minutes. The time begins when the performance begins, which may well be before the first utterance is made. A poet is certainly allowed several full seconds to adjust the microphone and get settled & ready, but as soon as s/he makes a connection with the audience ("Hey look, she's been standing there for 10 seconds and hasn't even moved"), the timekeeper can start the clock. The poet does not have an unlimited amount of "mime time." Poets with ambiguous beginnings and endings to their performances should seek out the timekeeper at each venue to settle on a starting & ending time. After three minutes, there is a 10-second grace period (up to and including 3:10:00). Starting at 3:10:01, a penalty is automatically deducted from each poet's overall score according to the following schedule:

3:10 and under	no penalty
3:10:01–3:20	−0.5
3:20:0–3:30	−1.0
3:30:01–3:40	−1.5
3:40:0–3:50	−2.0
and so on	[0.5 for every 10 seconds over 3:10]

(An additional 10 seconds is permitted in the finals without penalty.)

The announcement of the time penalty and its consequent deduction will be made by the emcee or scorekeeper after all the judges have reported their scores. The judges should not even be told that a poet went overtime until it is too late for them to adjust their scores.

Maximum Time Limit

After four minutes, only the emcee must stop a poet from continuing to perform.

Influencing the Crowd before the Bout Begins

Poets are allowed to talk casually with anyone in the crowd before the bout begins (except the judges, if they have already been chosen). They are not, however, allowed to give anything to the audience or have anyone do this for them. Furthermore, inside the venue (in the presence or within earshot of the audience) they must not act in any way that would make more of an impression than another competitor waiting for the competition to begin. Poets who violate this rule will be given one warning by the emcee, bout manager, or house manager. Further violation will result in a two-point penalty for that poet's score (or his team).

The Gag Rule

During any team member's individual performance, the remaining members of his or her team (including the coach and SlamMaster) must not lead, or otherwise teach the audience to respond to the performer in any way unless the performance has been designated as a team piece. The individual performer may attempt to elicit such responses from the audience, but his or her team should not help by offering anything other than laughter, and applause. Any team violating this rule during the preliminary rounds will have the offending poem designated as a team piece (by the emcee or bout manager, either publicly or privately later). If this happens during the individual semifinals or finals, the individual poet will be disqualified from the individual competition.

II. TEAMS & INDIVIDUALS

Team Eligibility

Teams must be chosen from an ongoing slam or reading series open to all poets regardless of age, sex, race, ability, appearance, or sexual orientation. All certified/registered venues are expected to uphold the Equal Opportunity Statement. Team members must be chosen through some form of competition; how that competition is structured is up to the local venue or SlamMaster so long as anyone who considers him/herself to be a part of the community fielding the slam team has the competitive opportunity to join it.

Because Poetry Slam is growing, not all certified venues can necessarily be included in the National Poetry Slam. To accommodate as many poets as possible, from as diverse a geographic base as can be achieved, some certified Poetry Slams will be encouraged to share an invitation to the National Poetry Slam. A person participating at the NPS can be a member of one and only one team.

Team Pieces

Duos, trios, quartets, and quintets (otherwise known as team, group, or collaborative pieces) are allowed, even encouraged, so long as all of the primary authors perform them. Refer to Section V (Definitions) for further clarification on primary authorship. The poet who offers up his individual spot on stage in order to accommodate a group piece must be one of the primary authors of that piece. Thus, a poet whose only appearance on stage during a bout is as part of a team piece must be one of the primary authors of that team piece.

A group piece with more than one primary author does not have to be used in the same primary author's slot each time it is performed in the course of the competition. But a group piece with only one primary author must only & always be performed during that writer/performer's slot. Group pieces may not be repeated in subsequent years unless all of the primary authors are present and on a team with one another again. The score of a team piece will be credited to the team as a whole, not to the primary author who offered up her individual turn on stage to accommodate it. Because team pieces do not receive rank scores in the bouts in which they are used, they do not affect the rank scores of individual poets in the same bout. In other words, even if a team piece receives the highest score in a bout, it will not receive the rank score of 1. The rank score of 1 goes to the highest-scoring individual poet of the bout.

A poet may render her/himself ineligible for consideration in the individual competition if s/he opts to use her/his team piece during a round in which poets are competing both as teams and as individuals. A team piece may be substituted for any or all of the members of a team in any bout. Provided all other rules regarding team pieces and repetition are followed, one team could use group pieces in each rotation.

The Use of Team Alternates

By the end of the registration period all teams must designate a minimum number of poets equal to the number of rotations in a preliminary bout and a maximum of 5. Teams may use their poets in any combination allowed by all other rules in their preliminary rounds so long as each team performs poems by different primary authors equal to at least the number of rotations in each bout. In elimination rounds, no individual poet may perform solo more than once, except in the case of a tiebreaker. There shall be no substitutions for registered team members after the end of the registration period. Any team violating this rule will be disqualified.

III. JUDGING & SCORING

Judging

All efforts shall be made to select five judges who will be fair. Once chosen, the judges will: 1) be given a set of printed instructions on how to judge a poetry slam, 2) have a private, verbal crash course by the emcee or bout manager on the dos and don'ts of poetry slam judging (where they can ask questions), and 3) hear the standardized Official Emcee

Spiel, which, among other things, will apprise the audience of their own responsibilities as well as remind the judges of theirs. Having heard, read, or otherwise experienced these three sets of instructions, a judge cannot be challenged over a score. Complaints, problems, and/or disagreements regarding the impartiality of the judges should be brought privately to the attention of the emcee or bout manager BE-FORE the bout begins. Having heard and understood the complaint, the bout manager or emcee will then make a decision (also privately) that cannot be further challenged.

Scoring

The judges will give each poem a score from 0 to 10, with 10 being the highest or "perfect" score. They will be encouraged to use one decimal place in order to preclude the likelihood of a tie. Each poem will get five scores. The high and the low scores will be dropped and the remaining three scores will be added together. Team scores will be displayed or otherwise publicly available during the bout.

Breaking Ties

If, at the conclusion of all rotations in a bout a tie exists for first place, each team tied for first place shall be required to send one more poem to the stage. It may be performed by any poet or poets on the teams who are tied. Teams in the tie breaker will draw for order. Judges will listen to all poems in the tie breaker rotation and at the conclusion of all poems, will assign a rank for each poem, starting with 1 for the best poem and increasing the rank by one for each additional poem in the rotation assigning each number exactly once (1 for the best, 2 for the second best, 3 for the third, etc.). The poem with the lowest total rank wins the tie breaker, and their team wins the bout.

If this results in another tie, judge preference will be used to determine the winner. Example: In a bout with a three-way tie see the table below:

	Poet A	Poet B	Poet C	Preference
	1	2	3	Poet A
	3	1	2	Poet B
	2	1	3	Poet B
	1	2	3	Poet A
	2	3	1	Poet A
Total	9	9	12	Poet A wins

Each poem performed in such a circumstance shall be subject to the "no repeat" rule. No ties for ranks lower than one shall be broken.

Normal time penalties apply but will be enforced in the following manner. Instead of a numeric half point penalty per ten seconds over time, one rank will be added for each ten seconds over time.

	Poet A	Poet B	Poet C	Preference
	1	2	3	Poet A
	3	1	2	Poet B
	2	1	3	Poet B
	1	2	3	Poet A
	2	3	1	Poet A
Time Penalty			1	
Time	9	9	13	Poet A wins

This process can possibly result in a second tie in a four-way tie. In that case, randomly eliminate the rank of one judge.

Ties in the Team Finals are not required to be broken. If a tie for first occurs on Finals night, the Bout Manager will confer with the coach or previously agreed upon representative for each team confidentially. If either of the teams elects to break the tie, the above is the procedure that they will use.

The same policies and procedures apply in regard to the Individual Finals, in which only ties for first will be eligible to be broken.

IV. OFFICIALS

Emcees.

The emcee will announce to the audience each poet's name and the team he is from. She will also require that all judges hold their scores up at the same time and that no judge changes his score after it is up. She is expected to move the show along quickly and keep the audience engaged and interested in the competition. Since she must be completely impartial, any witty banter directed at individual poets, poems, teams, or scores is inappropriate. Even genuine enthusiasm has to be carefully directed. The safest thing to do is encourage the audience to express their own opinions.

V. DEFINITIONS

Bout: a competition between two or more teams.

Order: the schematic that determines the order in which teams will read.

Primary Author(s): those writers/performers whose contributions to a particular group piece are so fundamental that they have at least as much of a right as any other writer/performer of the piece to claim ownership of it at any time. Primary authors must perform their pieces; if a writer/performer is watching other members of his team perform a group piece, then any contributions s/he might have made to it must not be significant enough to constitute primary authorship.

Prop: an object or article of clothing introduced into a performance with the effect of enhancing, illustrating, underscoring, or otherwise augmenting the words of the poem.

Rotation: when each team's first poet has read in a bout, the first rotation is over. There are as many rotations in a bout as there are opportunities for each team to perform.

Round: a complete set of bouts in which every team that is still eligible to compete does so. Eligibility to compete in successive rounds may be contingent upon success in earlier rounds.

Team Piece: a poem performed by two, three, four or all five members of the same team.

VI. SOME FAQS [FREQUENTLY ASKED QUESTIONS]

1. Can a team protest if they do not have enough working microphones on stage?

No, technical difficulties cannot be anticipated, nor can they be immediately fixed. For example, if a mic goes out during a performance it would probably be worse for the performer to have the tech person stop his/her performance to work on the mic.

DOCUMENT 2

The Official National Poetry Slam "Emcee Spiel"

This Is a Poetry Slam & This Is the Official "Emcee Spiel"

Ladies and Gentlemen, this is a Poetry Slam. My name is [say your name clearly] and I will be your emcee for the evening. The poetry slam is a competition invented in the 1980s by a Chicago construction worker named Marc Smith ["So what!"] in which performed poetry is judged by five members of the audience. Poets have three minutes to present their original work and may choose to do so accompanied by other members of their team. The judges will then score the piece anywhere from 0 to 10, evaluating such qualities as performance, content, and originality. The high and low scores of each performance are tossed, and the middle three are added giving the performer their score. Points are deducted for violating the three-minute time limit. We beseech the judges to remain unswayed by the audience—audience, try to sway the judges—and score each poet by the same set of criteria, ignoring whatever boisterous reaction your judgment elicits. Audience: Let the judges know how you feel about the job that they are doing, but be respectful in your exuberance; there could be no show without them. Now let me introduce you to the judges!

From *The Official 2007 Poetry Slam Rulebook*

DOCUMENT 3

The Official National Poetry Slam
Instructions for Judges

So You've Been Chosen to Judge a Poetry Slam

You have been enlisted in the service of poetry. This is supposed to be fun, and we don't expect you to be an expert, but we can offer certain guidelines that might make this more fun for everyone involved, especially you.

- We use the word "poem" to include text and performance. Some say you should assign a certain number of points for a poem's literary merit and a certain number of points for the poet's performance. Others feel that you are experiencing the poem only through the performance, and it may be impossible to separate the two. You will give each poem only one score.
- Trust your gut; and give the better poem the better score.
- Be fair. We all have our personal prejudices, but try to suspend yours for the duration of the slam. On the other hand, it's okay to have a prejudice that favors the true and the beautiful over the mundane and superficial, the original and enchanting over the boring and pedestrian.
- It's hard not to be influenced by the audience, but remember that in a quiet poem, the audience has no way to communicate what they're experiencing.
- The audience may boo you, that's their prerogative; as long as the better poem gets the better score, you're doing your job well.
- Be consistent with yourself. If you give the first poem a seven and the other judges give it a nine, that doesn't mean you should give the second poem a nine—unless it's a lot better than the first poem. In fact, if it's not as good as the first poem, we count on you to give it a lower score.
- Although the high and the low scores will be thrown out, don't ever make a joke out of your score thinking that it doesn't really matter.

A poem about geometry does not automatically deserve π as a score. Nor does one about failing a breathalyzer test deserve a 0.08.

- Your scores may rise as the night progresses. That's called "Score Creep." As long as you stay consistent, you're doing your job well.

The poets have worked hard to get here; treat them with respect. They are the show, not you (although there could be no show without you). All of us thank you for having the courage to put your opinions on the line.

Notes

INTRODUCTION

1. Joseph Epstein, "Who Killed Poetry?" *Commentary* 86, no. 2 (August 1988): 14–15.

2. Dana Gioia, "Can Poetry Matter?" in *Can Poetry Matter? Essays on Poetry and American Culture* (Saint Paul: Graywolf, 1992), 10, 19, 12.

3. Donald Hall, "Death to the Death of Poetry," Academy of American Poets Web site, http://www.poets.org/viewmedia.php/prmMID/16222. This piece was originally published in *Harper's* in 1989.

4. Richard Tillinghast, "American Poetry: Home Thoughts from Abroad," *Writer's Chronicle* 25, no. 5 (March–April 1993): 24.

5. Marc Smith, interview conducted at the 2002 National Poetry Slam, Minneapolis, by Susan B. A. Somers-Willett, August 16, 2002.

6. Marc Smith, "About Slam Poetry," in *Spoken Word Revolution: Slam, Hip-Hop, and the Poetry of a New Generation,* ed. Mark Eleveld (Naperville, IL: Sourcebooks MediaFusion, 2003), 117–18.

7. Jean Howard, "Performance Art, Performance Poetry: The Two Sisters," in *Spoken Word Revolution: Slam, Hip-Hop, and the Poetry of a New Generation,* ed. Mark Eleveld (Naperville, IL: Sourcebooks MediaFusion, 2003), 65–66.

8. Smith, interview.

9. Howard, "Performance Art," 65.

10. Both the Individual World Poetry Slam (iWPS) and the Women of the World Poetry Slam (WOWps) are relatively new competitions initiated in 2004 and 2008, respectively. Because both competitions are relatively new, my research represents the tournament records of the National Poetry Slam alone through 2007, which include both individual and team standings. It should be noted that, although they have slightly different tournament structures and rules, all three national competitions have many poems, poets, and organizers in common.

11. Marc Smith and Joe Kraynak, *The Complete Idiot's Guide to Slam Poetry* (New York: Alpha Books, 2004).

12. Marc Smith, "Slam Info: Philosophies," http://www.slampapi.com/new_site/background/philosophies.htm (accessed February 25, 2003).

13. Bob Holman, "The Room," in *Poetry Slam: The Competitive Art of Performance Poetry,* ed. Gary Mex Glazner (San Francisco: Manic D Press, 2000), 17.

14. Dana Gioia, *Disappearing Ink: Poetry at the End of Print Culture* (Saint Paul: Graywolf, 2004), 6–7.

15. Henry Louis Gates Jr., "Sudden Def," *New Yorker,* June 1995, 37.

16. Tyler Hoffman, "Treacherous Laughter: The Poetry Slam, Slam Poetry, and the Politics of Resistance," *Studies in American Humor* 3, no. 8 (2001): 49.

17. *Slamnation,* dir. Paul Devlin (1998; Slammin' Entertainment, 2004), DVD.

18. Roger Bonair-Agard, "In Memoriam: Sekou Sundiata," in *The National Poetry Slam 2007 Poet Guide* (Austin: National Poetry Slam Committee, 2007), 4.

19. Jeffrey McDaniel, "Slam and the Academy," in *Poetry Slam: The Competitive Art of Performance Poetry,* ed. Gary Mex Glazner (San Francisco: Manic D Press, 2000), 36.

20. "Poetry in Motion: Slam Dunking with Words," *Wall Street Journal,* September 10, 1998.

21. Genevieve Van Cleve, "Re: Slam," e-mail communication, October 30, 2001.

22. Maria Damon, "Was That 'Different,' 'Dissident,' or 'Dissonant'? Poetry (n) the Public Spear—Slams, Open Readings, and Dissident Traditions," in *Close Listening: Poetry and the Performed Word,* ed. Charles Bernstein (New York: Oxford University Press, 1998), 329–30.

23. The New York City poetry slam community has earned particular attention for its local flavor. For a discussion of its history, see Cristin O'Keefe Aptowicz, *Words in Your Face: A Guided Tour through Twenty Years of the New York City Poetry Slam* (New York: Soft Skull, 2008).

CHAPTER ONE

1. Dana Gioia, *Disappearing Ink: Poetry at the End of Print Culture* (Saint Paul: Graywolf , 2004), 7–10.

2. Charles Bernstein, ed., *Close Listening: Poetry and the Performed Word* (New York: Oxford University Press, 1998); Walter J. Ong, *Orality and Literature: The Technologizing of the Word* (New York: Methuen, 1982); Paul Zumthor, *Oral Poetry: An Introduction* (Minneapolis: University of Minnesota Press, 1990); Gregory Nagy, *Poetry as Performance: Homer and Beyond* (New York: Cambridge University Press, 1996).

3. Henry Taylor, "Read by the Author: Some Notes on Poetry in Performance," *Another Chicago Magazine* 32–33 (spring–summer 1997): 26.

4. This is not to say that rap lyrics are not to be considered formal verse; indeed, such lyrics are the most regularly metrical and rhymed type of poetry practiced in American culture today alongside children's verse. Nor is it to say that slam poets are uninformed about traditional poetic form and meter. I refer here specifically to the *tradition* cited by many slam poets in their use of formal devices. Especially recently, there has been a preponderance of rhymed, metered verse using the hip-hop idiom performed at the National Poetry Slam competition, a preponderance that may reflect the popularity and influence of programs such as *Russell Simmons Presents Def Poetry.* For further discussion of this use of language, see chapter 4.

5. Maria Damon, "Was That 'Different,' 'Dissident,' or 'Dissonant'? Poetry

(n) the Public Spear—Slams, Open Readings, and Dissident Traditions," in *Close Listening: Poetry and the Performed Word,* ed. Charles Bernstein (New York: Oxford University Press, 1998), 326.

6. Harold Bloom et al., "The Man in the Back Row Has a Question VI," *Paris Review* 154 (spring 2000): 379.

7. Luis J. Rodriguez, "Crossing Boundaries, Crossing Cultures: Poetry, Performance, and the New American Revolution," *Another Chicago Magazine* 32–33 (spring–summer 1997): 47.

8. Jack McCarthy, "Degrees of Difficulty," in *Spoken Word Revolution: Slam, Hip-Hop, and the Poetry of a New Generation,* ed. Mark Eleveld (Naperville, IL: Sourcebooks MediaFusion, 2003), 159.

9. Marc Smith, interview conducted at the 2002 National Poetry Slam, Minneapolis, by Susan B. A. Somers-Willett, August 16, 2002.

10. Marc Smith, "About Slam Poetry," in *Spoken Word Revolution: Slam, Hip-Hop, and the Poetry of a New Generation,* ed. Mark Eleveld (Naperville, IL: Sourcebooks MediaFusion, 2003), 116–17.

11. Taylor Mali, interview conducted at the 2002 National Poetry Slam, Minneapolis, by Susan B. A. Somers-Willett, August 15, 2002.

12. Marc Smith, "Slam Info: Philosophies," http://www.slampapi.com/new_site/background/philosophies.htm (accessed February 25, 2003).

13. Gioia, *Disappearing Ink,* 19.

14. McCarthy, "Degrees of Difficulty," 159.

15. John H. McWhorter, "Up from Hip-Hop," *Commentary* 115, no. 3 (2003): 63.

16. Henry Louis Gates Jr., "Sudden Def," *New Yorker,* June 1995, 40.

17. Smith, "About Slam Poetry," 118.

18. Bob Holman, "DisClaimer," in *Poetry Slam: The Competitive Art of Performance Poetry,* ed. Gary Mex Glazner (San Francisco: Manic D Press, 2000), 22.

19. The immediate exception here is interactive hypertexual poetry, whose order and composition are determined by its audience on a largely individual basis. Still, there are key differences that distinguish hypertextual and slam performance. One is that the relationship between author and audience via the Web is primarily textual or visual not performatively embodied as in the case of slam; another is that interactive hypertextual poetry defines its audience member as a "user" of the poem itself. Slam poetry, instead, is defined by the moment of delivery and the relationship between author and audience not that between poem and audience.

20. Lisa King, "Bring Them Back," in *Poetry Slam: The Competitive Art of Performance Poetry,* ed. Gary Mex Glazner (San Francisco: Manic D Press, 2000), 94.

21. *World's Greatest Poetry Slam, 2002* (Poetry Slam, Inc. and Wordsmith Press, 2003), DVD.

22. The description of competition given here is specific to the National Poetry Slam team competition in most recent years. The structure of the NPS tournament, as well as the number of teams competing in a bout, has changed over the years in order to accommodate more teams. The NPS, which used to sponsor both team and individual competition, has grown so large that after 2007 individual competition was discontinued in its ranks. In 2004, a new an-

nual event with a different tournament structure emerged for individual competitors under the auspices of Poetry Slam Incorporated, the Individual World Poetry Slam championship, and this event now operates independent of the NPS (i.e., it is held on different dates and in a different host city). The year 2008 ushered in a third PSI-sponsored tournament, also for individual competitors, called the Women of the World Poetry Slam. See appendix, document 1, for more information about NPS rules.

23. Danny Solis, "Aesthetics and Strategy of the Poetry Slam," in *Poetry Slam: The Competitive Art of Performance Poetry,* ed. Gary Mex Glazner (San Francisco: Manic D Press, 2000), 92.

24. Taylor Mali, *Top Secret Slam Strategies,* ed. Cristin O'Keefe Aptowicz (New York: Words Worth Ink and Wordsmith Press, 2001).

25. Gary Mex Glazner, "Poetry Slam: An Introduction," in *Poetry Slam: The Competitive Art of Performance Poetry,* ed. Gary Mex Glazner (San Francisco: Manic D Press, 2000), 11.

26. Jeremy Richards, "Redeeming the Spectacle: Poetry Slams and the Informed Judges Proposal," in *Poems from the Big Muddy: The 2004 National Poetry Slam Anthology,* ed. Cristin O'Keefe Aptowicz, Jeremy Richards, and Scott Woods (Whitmore Lake, MI: Wordsmith Press, 2004), 79.

27. See the Individual World Poetry Slam 2007 Web site, http://www.individualworldpoetryslam.com/index.html.

28. Smith, "About Slam Poetry," 119.

29. "Don't want to go to Austin or Chicago" refers to the fact that these were the host cities of the 1998 and 1999 National Poetry Slams, respectively.

30. Staceyann Chin, "I Don't Want to Slam," in *Poetry Slam: The Competitive Art of Performance Poetry,* ed. Gary Mex Glazner (San Francisco: Manic D Press, 2000), 206–7.

31. Billy Collins, "Poems on the Page, Poems in the Air," in *Spoken Word Revolution: Slam, Hip-Hop, and the Poetry of a New Generation,* ed. Mark Eleveld (Naperville, IL: Sourcebooks MediaFusion, 2003), 4. See also Peter Middleton, "The Contemporary Poetry Reading," in *Close Listening: Poetry and the Performed Word,* ed. Charles Bernstein (New York: Oxford University Press, 1998).

32. An exception to the NPS authorship rule is in the case of "sampling," where a poet may "incorporate, imitate, or otherwise 'signify on' the words, lyrics, or tune of someone else." Sampling usually materializes through the quotation and/or performance of song lyrics, although occasionally slam poets sample the style, tone, or writing of a competitor's poem in order to parody it. Sampling of the latter type has led to some prickly relationships between slam poets, and on a handful of occasions it has led to accusations of plagiarism. The NPS rules represent such controversies this way: "If [the slam poet] is only riffing off another's words, he should expect only healthy controversy; if on the other hand, he is ripping off their words, he should expect scornful contumely."

33. Saul Williams, "Amethyst Rocks," in *Spoken Word Revolution: Slam, Hip-Hop, and the Poetry of a New Generation,* ed. Mark Eleveld (Naperville, IL: Sourcebooks MediaFusion, 2003), 57.

34. Genevieve Van Cleve, "I Was the Worst Feminist in the World," in *Gas,*

Food, Lodging, Poetry: Poems by the 1997 Austin Slam Team (Austin: Gaslight Productions, 1997), 27.

35. Roland Barthes, "The Death of the Author," in *Image, Music, Text* (New York: Hill and Wang, 1978).

36. Tara Betts, "Rock 'n' Roll Be a Black Woman," in *Spoken Word Revolution: Slam, Hip-Hop, and the Poetry of a New Generation,* ed. Mark Eleveld (Naperville, IL: Sourcebooks MediaFusion, 2003), 47.

37. For a much more detailed discussion of African American blues women and their hallmarks, see Angela Y. Davis, *Blues Legacies and Black Feminism: Gertrude "Ma" Rainey, Bessie Smith, and Billie Holiday* (New York: Vintage, 1998).

38. Bob Holman, "Around and in the Scene," in *Spoken Word Revolution: Slam, Hip-Hop, and the Poetry of a New Generation,* ed. Mark Eleveld (Naperville, IL: Sourcebooks MediaFusion, 2003), 166.

39. Chin, "I Don't Want to Slam," 208–9.

CHAPTER TWO

1. The exception here is Black Arts poetry, a decidedly popular verse movement in which some poets blended avant-garde conventions with references to black popular culture in order to make them accessible to working-class and underclass black audiences. See James Smethurst, "'Pat Your Foot and Turn the Corner': Amiri Baraka, the Black Arts Movement, and the Poetics of a Popular Avant-Garde," *African American Review* 37, nos. 2–3 (2003): 261–70.

2. Joseph Harrington, *Poetry and the Public: The Social Form of Modern U.S. Poetics* (Middletown, CT: Wesleyan University Press, 2002), 11.

3. Ron Silliman, "Who Speaks? Ventriloquism and the Self in the Poetry Reading," in *Close Listening: Poetry and the Performed Word,* ed. Charles Bernstein (New York: Oxford University Press, 1998), 375, 366.

4. Stuart Hall, "Notes on Deconstructing 'The Popular'," in *People's History and Social Theory,* ed. Raphael Samuel (London: Routledge and Kegan Paul, 1981), 235.

5. Eric Lott, *Love and Theft: Blackface Minstrelsy and the American Working Class,* Race and American Culture Series (New York: Oxford University Press, 1993), 64.

6. For further reading on the concept of "black folk," see W. E. B. DuBois, *The Souls of Black Folk,* Dover Thrift unabridged ed. (New York: Dover, 1994).

7. *Oxford English Dictionary,* 2nd ed., s.v. "Minstrelsy."

8. Edward Le Roy Rice, *Monarchs of Minstrelsy: From "Daddy" Rice to Date* (New York: Kenny, 1911), 5, 11.

9. Dan Emmett was the author and original performer of "Dixie's Land," which became an anthem of the Confederate forces during the Civil War. Emmett, a native and lifetime resident of the North, wrote the song for the minstrel stage, and it was on the minstrel stage that it became popular in the South. Thus, it was popular audiences that, in an interesting twist of fate, de-

livered Emmett's song about a northern African American reminiscing about southern plantation life to the mouths of white southerners on Confederate battlefields.

10. Lott, *Love and Theft*, 20.

11. African American citizenship was not recognized until the Reconstruction period, when Congress ratified the Fourteenth Amendment to the Constitution in 1868. Still, public debate over issues regarding the practice and recognition of black citizenship (especially in the arenas of property ownership, voting rights, and education) continued well into the twentieth century. As a stage on which such issues played out, negotiating and parodying black citizenship continued to be a theme in minstrel performance after the Reconstruction era.

12. Simon Frith, *Sound Effects: Youth, Leisure, and the Politics of Rock 'n' Roll* (New York: Pantheon, 1981), 22–23.

13. James K. Kennard Jr., "Who Are Our National Poets?" *Knickerbocker* 26, no. 4 (1845): 332.

14. Ibid., 340.

15. See Robert C. Nowatzki, "'Our Only True National Poets': Blackface Minstrelsy and Cultural Nationalism," *American Transcendental Quarterly* 20, no. 1 (2006): 361–78.

16. Ralph Waldo Emerson, "The Poet," in *Selected Writings of Ralph Waldo Emerson,* ed. William H. Gilman (New York: Signet Classics, 2003).

17. *The Boys of New York End Men's Joke Book* (New York: Frank Tousey, 1898), 41. Material quoted from this book appears courtesy of the Harry Ransom Humanities Research Center, The University of Texas at Austin.

18. Lott, *Love and Theft*, 6.

19. Ibid., 6, 8. Homi Bhabha initially articulates this ambivalence of desire in his article "The Other Question: The Stereotype and Colonial Discourse," in *Visual Culture: The Reader,* ed. Jessica Evans and Stuart Hall (London: Sage, 1999). In Chapter 3, I propose that it is precisely this ambivalent desire that informs discourses of authenticity in slams.

20. William J. Mahar, *Behind the Burnt Cork Mask: Early Blackface Minstrelsy and Antebellum American Popular Culture,* Music in American Life Series (Urbana: University of Illinois Press, 1999).

21. Lott, *Love and Theft*, 51.

22. Albert Parry, *Garrets and Pretenders: A History of Bohemianism in America* (New York: Dover, 1960), 7.

23. Lott, *Love and Theft*, 51.

24. Allen Ginsberg, "When the Mode of the Music Changes, the Walls of the City Shake," in *Deliberate Prose: Selected Essays, 1952–1995,* ed. Bill Morgan (New York: HarperCollins, 2000), 248, 52.

25. Mark Eleveld, "Introduction," in *Spoken Word Revolution: Slam, Hip-Hop, and the Poetry of a New Generation,* ed. Mark Eleveld (Naperville, IL: Sourcebooks MediaFusion, 2003), 12.

26. Lee Hudson, "Poetics in Performance: The Beat Generation," in *Studies in Interpretation,* ed. Esther M. Doyle and Virginia Hastings Floyd (Amsterdam: Rodopi, 1977), 59.

27. Ann Charters, "Introduction: Variations on a Generation," in *The Portable Beat Reader,* ed. Ann Charters (New York: Penguin, 1992), xvii.

28. Allen Ginsberg, "A Definition of the Beat Generation," in *Deliberate Prose: Selected Essays, 1952–1995,* ed. Bill Morgan (New York: Harper-Collins, 2000), 236, Charters, "Introduction," xx–xxii.

29. Lorenzo Thomas, "Neon Griot: The Function of Poetry Readings in the Black Arts Movement," in *Close Listening: Poetry and the Performed Word,* ed. Charles Bernstein (New York: Oxford University Press, 1998), 306.

30. Allen Ginsberg, "The Six Gallery Reading," in *Deliberate Prose: Selected Essays, 1952–1995,* ed. Bill Morgan (New York: HarperCollins, 2000), 239–40.

31. Ginsberg, "Definition," 241.

32. Later in their writing careers, some Beats distinguished their work from white American culture by employing non-Western signifiers; the poets Phillip Whalen and Gary Snyder now explore Zen Buddhism and Eastern philosophy in their poetry.

33. Bruce Cook, *The Beat Generation* (New York: Charles Scribner's Sons, 1971), 223.

34. Lawrence Lipton, *The Holy Barbarians* (New York: Julian Messner, 1959), 93. For more about the popularity of rhythm and blues and its crossover to white audiences, see Andrew Ross, *No Respect: Intellectuals and Popular Culture* (New York: Routledge, 1989). See also Greil Marcus, *Mystery Train: Images of America in Rock 'n' Roll Music* (New York: Dutton, 1970).

35. Dore Ashton, *A Critical Study of Philip Guston* (Berkeley: University of California Press, 1990), 123. Thanks to Brett Boutwell for introducing me to these connections between art and music during this period.

36. Gregory Corso, "Variations on a Generation (excerpt)," in *The Portable Beat Reader,* ed. Ann Charters (New York: Penguin, 1992), 183.

37. Stephen E. Henderson, "Introduction: The Forms of Things Unknown," in *Understanding the New Black Poetry,* ed. Stephen Henderson (New York: William Morrow, 1973), 30.

38. Werner Sollors, *Amiri Baraka/LeRoi Jones: The Quest for a "Populist Modernism"* (New York: Columbia University Press, 1978), 24–25, 26, 27.

39. Norman Mailer, "The White Negro: Superficial Reflections on the Hipster," in *The Portable Beat Reader,* ed. Ann Charters (New York: Penguin, 1992), 586.

40. Ibid., 587.

41. Ross, *No Respect,* 81.

42. Jack Kerouac, *On the Road* (New York: Signet, 1957), 148.

43. Ross, *No Respect,* 68.

44. Ginsberg, "Definition," 239.

45. Ross, *No Respect,* 86.

46. Virginia Hiltz and Mike Sell, "The Black Arts Movement," English Department, University of Michigan, ENG 499 Course Web site, http://www.umich.edu/~eng499/ (accessed May 5, 2002).

47. Harold Cruse, *The Crisis of the Negro Intellectual* (New York: William Morrow, 1967).

48. Stephen E. Henderson, "Worrying the Line: Notes on Black American Poetry," in *The Line in Postmodern Poetry,* ed. Robert Frank and Henry Sayre (Chicago: University of Illinois Press, 1988), 63; Thomas, "Neon Griot," 314.

49. Thomas, "Neon Griot," 311.

50. Ibid., 312.

51. Stephen E. Henderson, "'Survival Motion': A Study of the Black Writer and the Black Revolution in America," in *The Militant Black Writer in Africa and the United States,* ed. Mercer Cook and Stephen E. Henderson (Madison: University of Wisconsin Press, 1969), 72. For a prominent example of black middle class synonymy with whiteness during this period, see Edward Franklin Frazier, *Black Bourgeoisie* (New York: Collier, 1962). Frazier's condemnation of this group is based on the argument that it gained economic security by conforming to white standards and sacrificing black identity.

52. Don L. Lee, "Toward a Definition: Black Poetry of the Sixties," in *The Black Aesthetic,* ed. Addison Gayle (Garden City: NY: Anchor/Doubleday, 1971), 223; Thomas, "Neon Griot," 311; and James Stewart, "The Development of the Black Revolutionary Artist," in *Black Fire: An Anthology of Afro-American Writing,* ed. LeRoi Jones and Larry Neal (New York: William Morrow, 1968), 7.

53. Larry Neal, "And Shine Swam On," in *Black Fire: An Anthology of Afro-American Writing,* ed. LeRoi Jones and Larry Neal (New York: William Morrow, 1968), 654.

54. Sollors, *Amiri Baraka,* 39, 29–30.

55. Stewart, "Development," 6.

56. Maulana Ron Karenga, "On Black Art," *Black Theater* 4 (1969): 9.

57. Amiri Baraka, *The LeRoi Jones/Amiri Baraka Reader,* ed. William J. Harris in collaboration with Amiri Baraka (New York: Thunder's Mouth, 1991), 219.

58. Henderson, "Introduction," 29; Sollors, *Amiri Baraka,* 36; Thomas, "Neon Griot," 308.

59. Henry Louis Gates Jr. and Nellie Y. McKay, eds., *The Norton Anthology of African American Literature* (New York: Norton, 1997), 1805.

60. Ibid.

61. Neal, "Shine," 653.

62. Henderson, "Introduction," 61.

63. Sollors, *Amiri Baraka,* 32; Hiltz and Sell, "Black Arts Movement."

64. Lee, "Toward a Definition," 223.

65. Gates and McKay, *Norton Anthology,* 1803.

66. Maulana Ron Karenga, "Black Cultural Nationalism," in *The Black Aesthetic,* ed. Addison Gayle (Garden City: NY: Anchor/Doubleday, 1971), 34.

67. Thomas, "Neon Griot," 309.

68. Sollors, *Amiri Baraka,* 94.

69. Neal, "Shine," 655.

70. Henderson, "Worrying the Line," 72; Thomas, "Neon Griot," 309–10, 17.

71. Henderson, "Introduction," 61; Geneviève Fabre, *Drumbeats, Masks, and Metaphor: Contemporary Afro-American Theater,* trans. Melvin Dixon (Cambridge: Harvard University Press, 1983), 66.

72. Karenga, "Black Cultural Nationalism."

73. Addison Gayle, "The Function of Black Literature at the Present Time," in *The Black Aesthetic,* ed. Addison Gayle (Garden City: NY: Anchor/Doubleday, 1971), 393.

74. Gates and McKay, *Norton Anthology,* 1797; Thomas, "Neon Griot," 312; Smethurst, "Pat Your Foot."

75. Phillip Brian Harper, *Are We Not Men?: Masculine Anxiety and the Problem of African-American Identity* (New York: Oxford University Press, 1996), 49.

76. Ibid., 53.

77. Hudson, "Poetics in Performance," 72–73.

78. Ross, *No Respect,* 67.

CHAPTER THREE

1. Shappy Seasholtz, "I Am That Nerd," in *Spoken Nerd* (New York: Little Vanity Press, 2002).

2. Genevieve Van Cleve, "Re: Slam," e-mail communication, October 30, 2001.

3. See my discussion of the theoretical and practical entanglements of authenticity in the introduction and later in this chapter. It is my position that authenticity, although performatively constructed and patently false, still has very real effects in culture because of the pervasive influence of realness in our everyday interactions. When using the word *authenticity* in this book, I mean to connote this understanding. Occasionally, I place the word in quotation marks to emphasize its constructed nature.

4. Erik Daniel, Debora Marsh, and Steve Marsh, eds., *The Official 2007 Poetry Slam Rulebook* (Lake Whitmore, MI: Wordsmith Press, 2007), 21.

5. Maria Damon, "Was That 'Different,' 'Dissident,' or 'Dissonant'? Poetry (n) the Public Spear—Slams, Open Readings, and Dissident Traditions," in *Close Listening: Poetry and the Performed Word,* ed. Charles Bernstein (New York: Oxford University Press, 1998), 329–30.

6. Ron Silliman, "Who Speaks? Ventriloquism and the Self in the Poetry Reading," in *Close Listening: Poetry and the Performed Word,* ed. Charles Bernstein (New York: Oxford University Press, 1998), 362.

7. Gayatri Chakravorty Spivak, "Can the Subaltern Speak?" in *Colonial Discourse and Post-colonial Theory: A Reader,* ed. Patrick Williams and Laura Chrisman (New York: Harvester Wheatsheaf, 1993).

8. For an excellent discussion of the phenomenon of racial fetishism, see "Reading Racial Fetishism: The Photographs of Robert Mapplethorpe," chapter 6 of Kobena Mercer, *Welcome to the Jungle: New Positions in Black Cultural Studies* (New York: Routledge, 1994).

9. John H. McWhorter, "Up from Hip-Hop," *Commentary* 115, no. 3 (2003): 63.

10. Elin Diamond, "Introduction," in *Performance and Cultural Politics,* ed. Elin Diamond (New York: Routledge, 1996), 5.

11. Erving Goffman, *The Presentation of Self in Everyday Life,* rev. ed. (New York: Anchor Books/Doubleday, 1959), 253.

12. J. L. Austin, *How to Do Things with Words,* ed. J. O. Urmson and Marina Sbisà, 2nd ed. (Cambridge: Harvard University Press, 1962).

13. See Diamond, "Introduction," 4–5.

14. See Andrew Parker and Eve Kosofsky Sedgwick, "Introduction," in *Performativity and Performance,* ed. Andrew Parker and Eve Kosofsky Sedgwick (New York: Routledge, 1995). See also Jon McKenzie, "Genre Trouble: (The) Butler Did It," in *The Ends of Performance,* ed. Peggy Phelan and Jill Lane (New York: New York University Press, 1998).

15. Judith Butler, *Bodies That Matter: On the Discursive Limits of "Sex"* (New York: Routledge, 1993), 12–13.

16. *Paris Is Burning,* dir. Jennie Livingston (1990; Off White Productions/Miramax, 2005), DVD.

17. See "Gender Is Burning: Questions of Appropriation and Subversion," chapter 4 of Butler, *Bodies That Matter.*

18. Diamond, "Introduction," 2.

19. Krystal Ashe, "[Slamsister] Big Poppas Original Post," Slamsisters Listserv, November 29, 2000, slamsister@yahoogroups.com. A wussy boy is Ott's self-crafted and self-proclaimed slam identity and is a masculinity defined by a heightened sensitivity to women's issues and his own self-conscious role as a white male. A wussy boy might, by traditional gender norms, be considered sensitive or effeminate for his behaviors.

20. Ragan Fox, "A Few Words on Identity . . . ," February 15, 2005, http://www.livejournal.com/community/slam_theory/1738.html.

21. Guy LeCharles Gonzalez, "Slam: Some Interesting Stats . . . ," National Poetry Slam Listserv, June 6, 2000, slam@datawranglers.com.

22. Michael Brown, "Slam Audience," e-mail communication, October 8, 2001.

23. *Slamnation,* dir. Devlin.

24. Krystal Ashe, discussion at the 2007 National Poetry Slam, Austin, personal communication, August 11, 2007.

25. The obvious example here is of Norman Mailer's hipster, who—as discussed in chapter 2—took his mantle from 1940s black jazz culture and whom Mailer characterized in as "the white Negro" in "The White Negro: Superficial Reflections on the Hipster," in *The Portable Beat Reader,* ed. Ann Charters (New York: Penguin, 1992). For a compelling history of hip and its ties to black music, see Andrew Ross, *No Respect: Intellectuals and Popular Culture* (New York: Routledge, 1989). For more on white consumption and appropriation of black style, see *Everything But the Burden: What White People Are Taking from Black Culture,* ed. Greg Tate (New York: Broadway Books, 2003).

26. Roger Bonair-Agard, "How Do We Spell Freedom," in *Burning Down the House: Selected Poems from the Nuyorican Poets Cafe's National Poetry Slam Champions,* Roger Bonair-Agard et al. (New York: Soft Skull, 2000), 39–43. For a performance of this poem in the slam context, see *The 2000 National Poetry Slam Finals* (Poetry Slam, Incorporated, and Wordsmith Press, 2001), DVD.

27. Gayle Danley, "Funeral Like Nixon's," in *Poetry Slam: The Competitive Art of Performance Poetry,* ed. Gary Mex Glazner (San Francisco: Manic D Press, 2000), 44.

28. Simon Frith, *Sound Effects: Youth, Leisure, and the Politics of Rock 'n' Roll* (New York: Pantheon, 1981), 23.

29. Ibid., 22, 23.

30. Taylor Mali, "How to Be a Political Poet," e-mail communication, July

29, 2002. For an audio recording of this poem, see track 14 of Taylor Mali's *Conviction* (Words Worth Ink and Wordsmith Press, 2003), CD.

31. Beau Sia, "An Open Letter to the Entertainment Industry," e-mail communication, June 24, 2007. For a performance of Sia's poem in the *Def Poetry* context, see *Russell Simmons Presents Def Poetry*, season 1, episode 3 (2002; HBO Video, 2004), DVD.

32. Amalia Ortiz, "Chicana Poet," e-mail Communication, 2 Aug 2007. For a performance of this poem in the slam context, see *The 2000 National Poetry Slam Finals* DVD.

33. "Me vale" is a Mexican expression that translates roughly as "I couldn't care less" or more strongly as "I don't give a damn."

34. Silliman, "Who Speaks?" 362–63.

35. Patricia Smith, *Big Towns, Big Talk* (Cambridge, MA: Zoland, 1992), 67–68. An audio version of Patricia Smith performing "Skinhead" can be accessed on the Internet at the E-Poet Network's "Book of Voices," http://voices.e-poets.net/SmithP. To view a performance in the *Def Poetry* context, see *Russell Simmons Presents Def Poetry*, season 2, episode 2 (2003; HBO Video, 2005), DVD.

36. Patricia Smith, "Persona Poem," in *Poetry Slam: The Competitive Art of Performance Poetry*, ed. Gary Mex Glazner (San Francisco: Manic D Press, 2000), 73.

37. Smith, *Big Towns*, 69.

CHAPTER FOUR

1. For more information about the slam's early venues and theatrical influences, see Jean Howard, "Performance Art, Performance Poetry: The Two Sisters," in *Spoken Word Revolution: Slam, Hip-Hop, and the Poetry of a New Generation*, ed. Mark Eleveld (Naperville, IL: Sourcebooks MediaFusion, 2003), 64–67.

2. Kobena Mercer, *Welcome to the Jungle: New Positions in Black Cultural Studies* (New York: Routledge, 1994), 240.

3. Imani Perry, *Prophets of the Hood: Politics and Poetics in Hip Hop* (Durham: Duke University Press, 2004), 39. For more on the issue of racial representation in hip-hop, see S. Craig Watkins, *Representing: Hip Hop Culture and the Production of Black Cinema* (Chicago: University of Chicago Press, 1998); S. Craig Watkins, *Hip Hop Matters: Politics, Pop Culture, and the Struggle for the Soul of a Movement* (Boston: Beacon, 2005); and Bakari Kitwana, *Why White Kids Love Hip-Hop: Wankstas, Wiggers, Wannabes, and the New Reality of Race in America* (New York: Basic Civitas, 2005).

4. In *The Crisis,* the official magazine of the NAACP, which he edited at the time, DuBois asserted that "real Negro theatre" should be "About us," "By us," "For us," and "Near us." See W. E. B. DuBois, "Krigwa Players Little Negro Theatre," *The Crisis,* July 1926, 134.

5. Wahneema Lubiano, "'But Compared to What?' Reading Realism, Representation, and Essentialism in *School Daze, Do the Right Thing,* and the Spike Lee Discourse," in *Representing Black Men,* ed. Marcellus Blount and George P. Cunningham (New York: Routledge, 1996), 186.

6. "The Grammy Awards," Infoplease.com/Pearson Education, http://www.infoplease.com/ipa/A0150533.html (accessed January 30, 2003).

7. Ray McNiece, "Just Call It Poetry," *Another Chicago Magazine* 32–33 (spring–summer 1997): 69–70.

8. Watkins, *Representing,* 179.

9. Ibid., 178.

10. Jerry Quickley, "Hip Hop Poetry," in *Spoken Word Revolution: Slam, Hip Hop, and the Poetry of a New Generation,* ed. Mark Eleveld (Naperville, IL: Sourcebooks MediaFusion, 2003), 42.

11. David Samuels, "The Rap on Rap: The 'Black Music' That Isn't Either," *New Republic,* November 11, 1991, 27.

12. Farai Chideya, "All Eyez on Us," *Time,* March 24, 1997, 24, 47.

13. Samuels, "Rap on Rap," 27.

14. Watkins, *Representing,* 187.

15. Ibid., 232.

16. Ibid., 237.

17. Quickley, "Hip Hop Poetry," 41–42.

18. Henry Louis Gates Jr., "Sudden Def," *New Yorker,* June 1995, 40–41.

19. Special thanks to the students in my spring 2005 Poetry and Performance course at the University of Illinois at Urbana-Champaign for helping me articulate these differences.

20. Saul Williams, *The Dead Emcee Scrolls: The Lost Teachings of Hip-Hop* (New York: MTV/Pocket Books, 2006), 173.

21. Marc Levin et al., "*Slam* Screenplay," in *Slam: The Screenplay and Filmmakers' Journals,* ed. Richard Stratton and Kim Wozencraft (New York: Grove, 1998), 266.

22. Eric Rudolph, "Shooting in the Big House: Documentary Techniques and Location Work Add Realism to the Prison Drama *Slam.,*" *American Cinematographer* 79, no. 2 (1998): 116.

23. John Kirby, "The Politics of Drama Vérité," in *Slam: The Screenplay and Filmmakers' Journals,* ed. Richard Stratton and Kim Wozencraft (New York: Grove, 1998), 145.

24. Andrew Higson, "Space, Place, Spectacle: Landscape and Townscape in the 'Kitchen Sink' Film," in *Dissolving Views: Key Writings on British Cinema,* ed. Andrew Higson (London: Cassel, 1996), 136.

25. Kirby, "Politics of Drama Vérité," 145, 46.

26. Marc Levin, "Dispatches from the Front: A Director's Journal," in *Slam: The Screenplay and Filmmakers' Journals,* ed. Richard Stratton and Kim Wozencraft (New York: Grove, 1998), 46.

27. Ibid., 28.

28. Levin et al., "*Slam* Screenplay," 261, 62.

29. J. L. Austin, *How to Do Things with Words,* ed. J. O. Urmson and Marina Sbisà, 2nd ed. (Cambridge: Harvard University Press, 1962).

30. Phillip Brian Harper, *Are We Not Men? Masculine Anxiety and the Problem of African-American Identity* (New York: Oxford University Press, 1996), 98.

31. "On spec" means that the production of *Slam* was not guaranteed release or distribution by a movie studio. *Slam* gained distribution from Trimark only after winning praise at the Sundance and Cannes film festivals.

32. Jeff Millar, "Improvisational 'Slam' Holds a Gritty Reality," *Houston Chronicle,* Star ed., October 23, 1998.

33. Greg Tate et al., "Fade to Black," *Village Voice,* December 15, 1998, 152.

34. Roger Ebert, "Prisoner Finds Rhyme and Reason in His Life," *The Record,* October 24, 1998.

35. Nicole Fleetwood, "Documenting 'the Real': Youth, Race, and the Discourse of Realness in Visual Culture," PhD diss., Stanford University, 2001, 105.

36. "Release Dates for *Slam,*" Internet Movie Database, http://us.imdb .com/ReleaseDates?0139615 (accessed February 9, 2003).

37. *Belly,* dir. Hype Williams (1998; Artisan, 2001), DVD.

38. Williams, *Dead Emcee Scrolls,* 169.

39. bell hooks, *Outlaw Culture: Resisting Representations* (New York: Routledge, 1994), 152.

40. Susan Berfield, "The CEO of Hip-Hop," *Business Week,* October 27, 2003.

41. Berfield, "CEO of Hip-Hop," 93. See also Bakari Kitwana, *The Hip-Hop Generation: Young Blacks and the Crisis in African American Culture* (New York: Basic Civitas, 2003).

42. "Who's Who in the Cast: Def Poetry Jam," *Playbill Theater Edition,* January 2003.

43. Watkins, *Representing,* 179, 272.

44. Pat Craig, "Simmons Keepin' It Real with 'Def Poetry Jam'," *Contra Costa Times,* June 21, 2002, Online ed. http://www.bayarea.com/mld/cc-times/3517020.htm.

45. Common examples include substituting the word *nizzle* for *nigger, scrizzle* for *scrilla* (cash), and *shizzle* for *shit.* The first use of this idiom appears to be Frankie Smith's 1981 song "Double Dutch Bus" (Dizzuble Dizzutch), and it has recently been picked up by prominent rappers such as Jay-Z and Snoop Dogg. Operating in a culture in which there is a premium on "flow" (the smooth transition from one lyric to another through improvisational rhyming), today's hip-hop artists no doubt have used this language to increase their capacity for improvisational rhyme. The growing popularity of "izzle" pig latin is also an inventive way for hip-hop artists to make their songs "clean" for the radio and music videos and to circumnavigate mandatory parental advisory warnings. In this respect, the use of *izzle* is strategic and profound; rappers have effectively reinvented their language to create a community of informed listeners and to subvert the recording industry's standards and policies regarding explicit lyrics.

46. *Russell Simmons Presents Def Poetry,* season 1, episode 3.

47. Tricia Rose, *Black Noise: Rap Music and Black Culture in Contemporary America,* Music/Culture Series (Middletown, CT: Wesleyan University Press, 1994), 17.

48. Sekou Andrews, "The Rapper," Blind Faith Records Web site, http://www.blindfaithrecords.com/rapper.html (accessed June 5, 2006). The original typography of the author's text has been retained here. Although Sekou's poem contains textual cues as to how he performs it (through the use of boldface, various type sizes and justifications, and italics), such orthogra-

phy and typography is not the norm in slam or spoken word poetry. In fact, few poets view their poetry on the page as a script for performance, and most would argue for the consumption of their work in *both* print and performance. As a hybrid brand of verse, such poetry deserves to be considered within and across these media, even though the relationship between a poem's performance and its appearance on the page can be frustratingly unclear (indeed, sometimes no relationship exists at all). In the absence of consensus on the issue, how a performance poem translates from page to stage is best left to a case-by-case analysis.

49. Bruce George, interview conducted at the Bowery Poetry Club, New York, by Susan B. A. Somers-Willett, July 14, 2002.

50. Danny Simmons, ed., *Russell Simmons Def Poetry Jam on Broadway . . . and More: The Choice Collection* (New York: Atria, 2003). The show ran from November 14, 2002, to May 4, 2003, at Broadway's Longacre Theater. It has also toured across the United States and Europe with a slightly different cast.

51. "Who's Who in the Cast."

52. Jill Dolan, *Utopia in Performance: Finding Hope at the Theater* (Ann Arbor: University of Michigan Press, 2005), 107.

53. These observations are drawn from a *Def Poetry Jam on Broadway* performance that I attended on January 3, 2003.

54. John H. McWhorter, "Up from Hip-Hop," *Commentary* 115, no. 3 (2003): 63–64.

55. Dolan, *Utopia in Performance,* 92.

56. Phillip Hopkins, "Russell Simmons Def Poetry Jam on Broadway," TheaterMania.com, November 15, 2002, http://www.theatermania.com/news/reviews/index.cfm?story=2789&cid=1.

57. Martin Denton, "Def Poetry Jam on Broadway," NYTheatre.com, November 19, 2002, http://www.nytheatre.com/nytheatre/def.htm.

58. James Sullivan, "Uplifting Hip-Hop Show Really Tells It Like It Is: Well-Versed Poets Are Funny and Earthy in 'Def Poetry Jam'," *San Francisco Chronicle,* June 27, 2002.

59. Jon Pareles, "A New Platform for the New Poets," *New York Times,* November 10, 2002.

60. Ibid.

61. Simmons, *Russell Simmons Def Poetry Jam on Broadway,* 119–20.

62. Ibid., 102. For a performance of "Front Page" in the *Def Poetry* context, see *Russell Simmons Presents Def Poetry,* season 1, episode 1 (2002; HBO Video, 2004), DVD. To hear Black Ice performing this poem as a hip-hop track, see track 8 of Lamar Manson [Black Ice], *The Death of Willie Lynch,* Koch Records, 2006, CD.

63. Simmons, *Russell Simmons Def Poetry Jam on Broadway,* 22. For a performance of "410 Days in the Life," see *Russell Simmons Presents,* season 2, episode 2.

64. Simmons, *Russell Simmons Def Poetry Jam on Broadway,* 39, 40.

65. Ibid., 4.

66. Leslie Katz, "Universal Language of Poetry," *San Francisco Examiner,* July 17, 2002.

67. *Slam Planet: War of the Words,* dir. Mike Henry and Kyle Fuller (2006; Slam Channel, 2006).

68. Chaka Ferguson, "Rap Mogul Simmons Takes Poetry Mainstream with HBO Series," *Augusta Chronicle,* March 25, 2002.

69. George, interview.

70. Ben Brantley, "Untamed Poetry, Loose Onstage," *New York Times,* November 15, 2002.

71. By "selling out," I mean to conjure both the idea of selling out performance venues and the common accusation that mainstream artists have to sell out their political interests to the music industry to achieve commercial success.

72. Staceyann Chin, "Almost Famous: An Original Broadway Def Poetry Jam Cast Member Learns That the Trick Is to Survive after the Stage Lights Go Down," *Black Issues Book Review,* March–April 2004.

73. Amy Robinson, "Forms of Appearance Value: Homer Plessy and the Politics of Privacy," in *Performance and Cultural Politics,* ed. Elin Diamond (New York: Routledge, 1996), 251.

74. Alix Olson, "Diary of a Slam Poet," *Ms.,* December–January 2000, 69.

75. Gareth Griffiths, "The Myth of Authenticity," in *The Post-colonial Studies Reader,* ed. Bill Ashcroft, Gareth Griffiths, and Helen Tiffin (New York: Routledge, 1995), 241.

76. Jeanette Brown, "Perry Ellis Is Talking Up Poetry," *Business Week,* November 23, 1998.

77. Elana Ashanti Jefferson, "Def Jam Poetry Hip-Hops into Denver's Spotlight," *Denver Post,* January 16, 2005, F1.

78. Rose, *Black Noise,* 17.

79. Ibid., 19.

80. Denton, "Def Poetry Jam on Broadway."

81. Craig, "Simmons Keepin' It Real."

82. Samuels, "Rap on Rap," 29.

83. Ibid.

84. Eric Lott, *Love and Theft: Blackface Minstrelsy and the American Working Class,* Race and American Culture Series (New York: Oxford University Press, 1993), 39.

EPILOGUE

1. John Barr, "American Poetry in the New Century," *Poetry* 188, no. 5 (September 2006): 433–41.

2. Victor Turner, *The Anthropology of Performance* (New York: Performing Arts Journal Publications, 1987), 24.

3. Ron Silliman, "Who Speaks? Ventriloquism and the Self in the Poetry Reading," in *Close Listening: Poetry and the Performed Word,* ed. Charles Bernstein (New York: Oxford University Press, 1998), 362.

Bibliography

Algarín, Miguel, and Bob Holman, eds. *Aloud: Voices from the Nuyorican Poets Cafe.* New York: Owl-Holt, 1994.

Andrews, Sekou. "The Rapper." Blind Faith Records Web site, http://www.blindfaithrecords.com/rapper.html (accessed June 5, 2006).

Anglesey, Zoë, ed. *Listen Up! Spoken Word Poetry.* New York: One World–Ballantine, 1999.

Aptowicz, Cristin O'Keefe. *Words in Your Face: A Guided Tour through Twenty Years of the New York City Poetry Slam.* New York: Soft Skull, 2008.

Ashe, Krystal. Discussion at the 2007 National Poetry Slam, Austin. Personal communication, August 11, 2007.

Ashe, Krystal. "[Slamsister] Big Poppas Original Post." Slamsisters Listserv, November 29, 2000, slamsister@yahoogroups.com.

Ashton, Dore. *A Critical Study of Philip Guston.* Berkeley: University of California Press, 1990.

Austin, J. L. *How to Do Things with Words.* Ed. J. O. Urmson and Marina Sbisà. 2nd ed. Cambridge: Harvard University Press, 1962.

Baraka, Amiri. *The LeRoi Jones/Amiri Baraka Reader.* Ed. William J. Harris in collaboration with Amiri Baraka. New York: Thunder's Mouth, 1991.

Barr, John. "American Poetry in the New Century." *Poetry* 188, no. 5 (September 2006): 433–41.

Barthes, Roland. "The Death of the Author." In *Image, Music, Text,* 142–48. New York: Hill and Wang, 1978.

Belly. Dir. Hype Williams. 1998; Artisan, 2001. DVD.

Bentson, Kimberly W. *Performing Blackness: Enactments of African-American Modernism.* New York: Routledge, 2000.

Berfield, Susan. "The CEO of Hip-Hop." *Business Week,* October 27, 2003, 90–98.

Bernstein, Charles, ed. *Close Listening: Poetry and the Performed Word.* New York: Oxford University Press, 1998.

Betts, Tara. "Rock 'n' Roll Be a Black Woman." In *Spoken Word Revolution: Slam, Hip-Hop, and the Poetry of a New Generation,* ed. Mark Eleveld, 47–48. Naperville, IL: Sourcebooks MediaFusion, 2003.

Bhabha, Homi. "The Other Question: The Stereotype and Colonial Discourse." In *Visual Culture: The Reader,* ed. Jessica Evans and Stuart Hall, 370–78. London: Sage, 1999.

Bloom, Harold, David Barber, Stephen Burt, Frank Kermode, Richard Lamb, William Logan, David Mendelsohn, Richard Poirier, and Helen Vendler.

"The Man in the Back Row Has a Question VI." *Paris Review* 154 (spring 2000): 370–402.

Bonair-Agard, Roger. "How Do We Spell Freedom." In *Burning Down the House: Selected Poems from the Nuyorican Poets Cafe's National Poetry Slam Champions,* Roger Bonair-Agard et al., 39–43. New York: Soft Skull, 2000.

Bonair-Agard, Roger. "In Memoriam: Sekou Sundiata." In *The National Poetry Slam 2007 Poet Guide,* 4–5. Austin: National Poetry Slam Committee, 2007.

Boys N the Hood. Dir. John Singleton. 1991; Columbia, 1998. DVD.

The Boys of New York End Men's Joke Book. New York: Frank Tousey, 1898.

Brantley, Ben. "Untamed Poetry, Loose Onstage." *New York Times,* November 15, 2002, 1.

Brooks, Gwendolyn. "For Those of My Sisters Who Kept Their Naturals." In *Primer for Blacks,* 4–5. Chicago: Third World Press, 1980.

Brown, Jeanette. "Perry Ellis Is Talking Up Poetry." *Business Week,* November 23, 1998, 8.

Brown, Michael. "Slam Audience." E-mail communication, October 8, 2001.

Butler, Judith. *Bodies That Matter: On the Discursive Limits of "Sex."* New York: Routledge, 1993.

Charters, Ann. "Introduction: Variations on a Generation." In *The Portable Beat Reader,* ed. Ann Charters, xv–xxxvi. New York: Penguin, 1992.

Chideya, Farai. "All Eyez on Us." *Time,* March 24, 1997, 24, 47.

Chin, Staceyann. "Almost Famous: An Original Broadway Def Poetry Jam Cast Member Learns That the Trick Is to Survive after the Stage Lights Go Down." *Black Issues Book Review,* March–April, 2004.

Chin, Staceyann. "I Don't Want to Slam." In *Poetry Slam: The Competitive Art of Performance Poetry,* ed. Gary Mex Glazner, 206–9. San Francisco: Manic D Press, 2000.

Collins, Billy. "Poems on the Page, Poems in the Air." In *Spoken Word Revolution: Slam, Hip-Hop, and the Poetry of a New Generation,* ed. Mark Eleveld, 3–5. Naperville, IL: Sourcebooks MediaFusion, 2003.

Cook, Bruce. *The Beat Generation.* New York: Charles Scribner's Sons, 1971.

Corso, Gregory. "Variations on a Generation (excerpt)." In *The Portable Beat Reader,* ed. Ann Charters, 182–85. New York: Penguin, 1992.

Craig, Pat. "Simmons Keepin' It Real with 'Def Poetry Jam'." *Contra Costa Times,* June 21, 2002. Online ed., http://www.bayarea.com/mld/cctimes/3517020.htm.

Cruse, Harold. *The Crisis of the Negro Intellectual.* New York: William Morrow, 1967.

Damon, Maria. "Was That 'Different,' 'Dissident,' or 'Dissonant'? Poetry (n) the Public Spear—Slams, Open Readings, and Dissident Traditions." In *Close Listening: Poetry and the Performed Word,* ed. Charles Bernstein, 324–42. New York: Oxford University Press, 1998.

Daniel, Erik, Debora Marsh, and Steve Marsh, eds. *The Official 2007 Poetry Slam Rulebook.* Whitmore Lake, MI: Wordsmith Press, 2007.

Danley, Gayle. "Funeral Like Nixon's." In *Poetry Slam: The Competitive Art of Performance Poetry,* ed. Gary Mex Glazner, 42–44. San Francisco: Manic D Press, 2000.

Davis, Angela Y. *Blues Legacies and Black Feminism: Gertrude "Ma" Rainey, Bessie Smith, and Billie Holiday.* New York: Vintage, 1998.

Del Valle, Mayda. "Tongue Tactics." In *Russell Simmons Presents Def Poetry Jam on Broadway . . . and More,* ed. Danny Simmons, 145–49. New York: Atria, 2003.

Denton, Martin. "Def Poetry Jam on Broadway." NYTheatre.com, November 19, 2002, http://www.nytheatre.com/nytheatre/def.htm.

Diamond, Elin. "Introduction." In *Performance and Cultural Politics,* ed. Elin Diamond, 1–12. New York: Routledge, 1996.

Dolan, Jill. *Utopia in Performance: Finding Hope at the Theater.* Ann Arbor: University of Michigan Press, 2005.

"DPJ Roots: Quotes on Def Poetry Jam." http://www.defpoetryjam.com/DPJ roots.htm (accessed December 3, 2003).

DuBois, W. E. B. "Krigwa Players Little Negro Theatre." *The Crisis,* July 1926, 134–36.

DuBois, W. E. B. *The Souls of Black Folk.* Dover Thrift unabridged ed. New York: Dover, 1994.

Ebert, Roger. "Prisoner Finds Rhyme and Reason in His Life." *The Record,* October 24, 1998.

Elam, Harry J., Jr., and Kennell Jackson, ed. *Black Cultural Traffic: Crossroads in Global Performance and Popular Culture.* Ann Arbor: University of Michigan Press, 2005.

Eleveld, Mark. "Introduction." In *Spoken Word Revolution: Slam, Hip-Hop, and the Poetry of a New Generation,* ed. Mark Eleveld, 10–12. Naperville, IL: Sourcebooks MediaFusion, 2003.

Eleveld, Mark, ed. *The Spoken Word Revolution Redux.* Naperville, IL: Sourcebooks MediaFusion, 2007.

Eleveld, Mark, ed. *The Spoken Word Revolution: Slam, Hip-Hop, and the Poetry of a New Generation.* Naperville, IL: Sourcebooks MediaFusion, 2003.

Emerson, Ralph Waldo. "The Poet." In *Selected Writings of Ralph Waldo Emerson,* ed. William H. Gilman, 325–49. New York: Signet Classics, 2003.

Epstein, Joseph. "Who Killed Poetry?" *Commentary* 86, no. 2 (August 1988): 13–20.

Evans, Mari. "I Am a Black Woman." In *The Norton Anthology of African American Literature,* ed. Henry Louis Gates Jr. and Nellie Y. McKay, 1808. New York: Norton, 1997.

Fabre, Geneviève. *Drumbeats, Masks, and Metaphor: Contemporary Afro-American Theater.* Trans. Melvin Dixon. Cambridge: Harvard University Press, 1983.

Ferguson, Chaka. "Rap Mogul Simmons Takes Poetry Mainstream with HBO Series." *Augusta Chronicle,* March 25, 2002. Online ed., http://www.au gustachronicle.com/stories/032502/fea_124-7016.shtml.

Fighting Words. Dir. E. Paul Edwards. 2007; Indican, 2007. DVD.

Fleetwood, Nicole. "Documenting "the Real": Youth, Race, and the Discourse of Realness in Visual Culture." PhD diss., Stanford University, 2001.

Fox, Ragan. "A Few Words on Identity. . . ," February 15, 2005. http://www .livejournal.com/community/slam_theory/1738.html.

Fox, Ragan. "To Be Straight." In *Heterophobia,* 51–52. Maple Shade, NJ: Lethe, 2005.

Frazier, Edward Franklin. *Black Bourgeoisie*. New York: Collier, 1962.

Frith, Simon. *Sound Effects: Youth, Leisure, and the Politics of Rock 'n' Roll*. New York: Pantheon, 1981.

Gates, Henry Louis, Jr. "Sudden Def." *New Yorker*, June 1995, 34–42.

Gates, Henry Louis, Jr., and Nellie Y. McKay, eds. *The Norton Anthology of African American Literature*. New York: Norton, 1997.

Gayle, Addison. "The Function of Black Literature at the Present Time." In *The Black Aesthetic*, ed. Addison Gayle, 383–94. Garden City: NY: Anchor/Doubleday, 1971.

George, Bruce. Interview conducted at the Bowery Poetry Club, New York, by Susan B. A. Somers-Willett, July 14, 2002.

Ginsberg, Allen. "A Definition of the Beat Generation." In *Deliberate Prose: Selected Essays, 1952–1995*, ed. Bill Morgan, 236–39. New York: HarperCollins, 2000.

Ginsberg, Allen. "The Six Gallery Reading." In *Deliberate Prose: Selected Essays 1952–1995*, ed. Bill Morgan, 239–42. New York: HarperCollins, 2000.

Ginsberg, Allen. "When the Mode of the Music Changes, the Walls of the City Shake." In *Deliberate Prose: Selected Essays, 1952–1995*, ed. Bill Morgan, 247–54. New York: HarperCollins, 2000.

Gioia, Dana. "Can Poetry Matter?" In *Can Poetry Matter? Essays on Poetry and American Culture*, 1–24. Saint Paul: Graywolf, 1992.

Gioia, Dana. *Disappearing Ink: Poetry at the End of Print Culture*. Saint Paul: Graywolf, 2004.

Glazner, Gary Mex. "Poetry Slam: An Introduction." In *Poetry Slam: The Comprehensive Art of Performance Poetry*, ed. Gary Mex Glazner, 11–12 San Francisco, Manic D Press, 2000.

Glazner, Gary Mex, ed. *Poetry Slam: The Competitive Art of Performance Poetry*. San Francisco: Manic D Press, 2000.

Goffman, Erving. *The Presentation of Self in Everyday Life*. Rev. ed. New York: Anchor Books/Doubleday, 1959.

Golden, Thelma, ed. *Black Male: Representations of Masculinity in Contemporary American Art*. New York: Whitney Museum of American Art, 1994.

Gonzalez, Guy LeCharles. "Slam: Some Interesting Stats . . ." National Poetry Slam Listserv, June 6, 2000, slam@datawranglers.com.

"The Grammy Awards." Infoplease.com/Pearson Education, http://www.info please.com/ipa/A0150533.html (accessed January 30, 2003).

Griffiths, Gareth. "The Myth of Authenticity." In *The Post-colonial Studies Reader*, ed. Bill Ashcroft, Gareth Griffiths, and Helen Tiffin, 237–41. New York: Routledge, 1995.

Hall, Donald. "Death to the Death of Poetry." Academy of American Poets Web site, http://www.poets.org/viewmedia.php/prmMID/16222. Originally published in *Harper's* (September 1989): 72–76.

Hall, Stuart. "Notes on Deconstructing 'The Popular'." In *People's History and Social Theory*, ed. Raphael Samuel, 227–39. London: Routledge and Kegan Paul, 1981.

Harper, Phillip Brian. *Are We Not Men? Masculine Anxiety and the Problem of African-American Identity*. New York: Oxford University Press, 1996.

Harrington, Joseph. *Poetry and the Public: The Social Form of Modern U.S. Poetics*. Middletown, CT: Wesleyan University Press, 2002.

Henderson, Stephen E. "Introduction: The Forms of Things Unknown." In *Understanding the New Black Poetry: Black Speech and Black Music as Poetic References,* ed. Stephen Henderson, 1–70. New York: William Morrow, 1973.

Henderson, Stephen E. "'Survival Motion': A Study of the Black Writer and the Black Revolution in America." In *The Militant Black Writer in Africa and the United States,* ed. Mercer Cook and Stephen E. Henderson, 63–129. Madison: University of Wisconsin Press, 1969.

Henderson, Stephen E. "Worrying the Line: Notes on Black American Poetry." In *The Line in Postmodern Poetry,* ed. Robert Frank and Henry Sayre, 60–82. Chicago: University of Illinois Press, 1988.

Higson, Andrew. "Space, Place, Spectacle: Landscape and Townscape in the 'Kitchen Sink' Film." In *Dissolving Views: Key Writings on British Cinema,* ed. Andrew Higson, 133–56. London: Cassel, 1996.

Hiltz, Virginia, and Mike Sell. "The Black Arts Movement." English Department, University of Michigan, ENG 499 Course Web site, http://www.umich.edu/~eng499/ (accessed May 5, 2002).

Hoffman, Tyler. "Treacherous Laughter: The Poetry Slam, Slam Poetry, and the Politics of Resistance." *Studies in American Humor* 3, no. 8 (2001): 49–64.

Holman, Bob. "Around and in the Scene." In *Spoken Word Revolution: Slam, Hip-Hop, and the Poetry of a New Generation,* ed. Mark Eleveld, 165–67. Naperville, IL: Sourcebooks MediaFusion, 2003.

Holman, Bob. "DisClaimer." In *Poetry Slam: The Competitive Art of Performance Poetry,* ed. Gary Mex Glazner, 22. San Francisco: Manic D Press, 2000.

Holman, Bob. "Praise Poem for Slam: Why Slam Causes Pain and Is a Good Thing." In *Spoken Word Revolution: Slam, Hip-Hop, and the Poetry of a New Generation,* ed. Mark Eleveld, 169–70. Naperville, IL: Sourcebooks MediaFusion, 2003.

Holman, Bob. "The Room." In *Poetry Slam: The Competitive Art of Performance Poetry,* ed. Gary Mex Glazner, 15–21. San Francisco: Manic D Press, s2000.

hooks, bell. *Outlaw Culture: Resisting Representations.* New York: Routledge, 1994.

Hopkins, Phillip. "Russell Simmons Def Poetry Jam on Broadway." TheaterMania.com, November 15, 2002, http://www.theatermania.com/news/reviews/index.cfm?story=2789&cid=1.

Howard, Jean. "Performance Art, Performance Poetry: The Two Sisters." In *Spoken Word Revolution: Slam, Hip-Hop, and the Poetry of a New Generation,* ed. Mark Eleveld, 64–67. Naperville, IL: Sourcebooks MediaFusion, 2003.

Hudson, Lee. "Poetics in Performance: The Beat Generation." In *Studies in Interpretation,* ed. Esther M. Doyle and Virginia Hastings Floyd, 59–76. Amsterdam: Rodopi, 1977.

Individual World Poetry Slam 2007 Web site, http://www.individualworldpoetryslam.com/index.html.

Jefferson, Elana Ashanti. "Def Jam Poetry Hip-Hops into Denver's Spotlight." *Denver Post,* January 16, 2005, F1.

Johnson, E. Patrick. *Appropriating Blackness: Performance and the Politics of Authenticity.* Durham: Duke University Press, 2003.

Karenga, Maulana Ron. "Black Cultural Nationalism." In *The Black Aesthetic,* ed. Addison Gayle, 31–37. Garden City: NY: Anchor/Doubleday, 1971.

Karenga, Maulana Ron. "On Black Art." *Black Theater* 4 (1969): 9–10.

Katz, Leslie. "Universal Language of Poetry." *San Francisco Examiner,* July 17, 2002.

Kennard, James K., Jr. "Who Are Our National Poets?" *Knickerbocker* 26, no. 4 (1845): 331–41.

Kerouac, Jack. *On the Road.* New York: Signet, 1957.

King, Lisa. "Bring Them Back." In *Poetry Slam: The Competitive Art of Performance Poetry,* ed. Gary Mex Glazner, 93–94. San Francisco: Manic D Press, 2000.

Kirby, John. "The Politics of Drama Vérité." In *Slam: The Screenplay and Filmmakers' Journals,* ed. Richard Stratton and Kim Wozencraft, 144–46. New York: Grove, 1998.

Kitwana, Bakari. *The Hip-Hop Generation: Young Blacks and the Crisis in African American Culture.* New York: Basic Civitas, 2003.

Kitwana, Bakari. *Why White Kids Love Hip-Hop: Wankstas, Wiggers, Wannabes, and the New Reality of Race in America.* New York: Basic Civitas, 2005.

Lee, Don L. "Toward a Definition: Black Poetry of the Sixties." In *The Black Aesthetic,* ed. Addison Gayle, 222–33. Garden City: NY: Anchor/Doubleday, 1971.

Levin, Marc. "Dispatches from the Front: A Director's Journal." In *Slam: The Screenplay and Filmmakers' Journals,* ed. Richard Stratton and Kim Wozencraft, 23–47. New York: Grove, 1998.

Levin, Marc, Bonz Malone, Sonja Sohn, Richard Stratton, and Saul Williams. "*Slam* Screenplay." In *Slam: The Screenplay and Filmmakers' Journals,* ed. Richard Stratton and Kim Wozencraft, 171–266. New York: Grove, 1998.

Lipton, Lawrence. *The Holy Barbarians.* New York: Julian Messner, 1959.

Lott, Eric. *Love and Theft: Blackface Minstrelsy and the American Working Class.* Race and American Culture Series. New York: Oxford University Press, 1993.

Lubiano, Wahneema. "'But Compared to What?' Reading Realism, Representation, and Essentialism in *School Daze, Do the Right Thing,* and the Spike Lee Discourse." In *Representing Black Men,* ed. Marcellus Blount and George P. Cunningham, 173–204. New York: Routledge, 1996.

Mahar, William J. *Behind the Burnt Cork Mask: Early Blackface Minstrelsy and Antebellum American Popular Culture.* Music in American Life Series. Urbana: University of Illinois Press, 1999.

Mailer, Norman. "The White Negro: Superficial Reflections on the Hipster." In *The Portable Beat Reader,* ed. Ann Charters, 581–605. New York: Penguin, 1992.

Maira, Sunaina, and Elizabeth Soep, ed. *Youthscapes: The Popular, the National, the Global.* Philadelphia: University of Pennsylvania Press, 2005.

Mali, Taylor. *Conviction.* Words Worth Ink and Wordsmith Press, 2003. CD.

Mali, Taylor. "How to Be a Political Poet." E-mail communication, July 29, 2002.

Mali, Taylor. Interview conducted at the 2002 National Poetry Slam, Minneapolis, by Susan B. A. Somers-Willett, August 15, 2002.

Mali, Taylor. *Top Secret Slam Strategies.* Ed. Cristin O'Keefe Aptowicz. New York: Words Worth Ink and Wordsmith Press, 2001.

Manson, Lamar [Black Ice]. *The Death of Willie Lynch.* Koch Records, 2006. CD.

Marcus, Greil. *Mystery Train: Images of America in Rock 'n' Roll Music.* New York: Dutton, 1970.

McCarthy, Jack. "Degrees of Difficulty." In *Spoken Word Revolution: Slam, Hip-Hop, and the Poetry of a New Generation,* ed. Mark Eleveld, 159–60. Naperville, IL: Sourcebooks MediaFusion, 2003.

McClure, Michael. *Scratching the Beat Surface.* San Francisco: North Point Press, 1982.

McDaniel, Jeffrey. "Slam and the Academy." In *Poetry Slam: The Competitive Art of Performance Poetry,* ed. Gary Mex Glazner, 35–37. San Francisco: Manic D Press, 2000.

McKenzie, Jon. "Genre Trouble: (The) Butler Did It." In *The Ends of Performance,* ed. Peggy Phelan and Jill Lane, 217–35. New York: New York University Press, 1998.

McNiece, Ray. "Just Call It Poetry." *Another Chicago Magazine* 32–33 (spring–summer 1997): 69–70.

McWhorter, John H. "Up from Hip-Hop." *Commentary* 115, no. 3 (2003): 62–65.

Medina, Tony, and Louis Reyes Rivera, eds. *Bum Rush the Page: A Def Poetry Jam.* New York: Three Rivers Press, 2001.

Menace II Society. Dir. Albert Hughes and Allen Hughes. 1993; New Line Cinema, 1997. DVD.

Mercer, Kobena. *Welcome to the Jungle: New Positions in Black Cultural Studies.* New York: Routledge, 1994.

Middleton, Peter. "The Contemporary Poetry Reading." In *Close Listening: Poetry and the Performed Word,* ed. Charles Bernstein, 262–99. New York: Oxford University Press, 1998.

Millar, Jeff. "Improvisational 'Slam' Holds a Gritty Reality." *Houston Chronicle,* Star ed., October 23, 1998, 6.

Nagy, Gregory. *Poetry as Performance: Homer and Beyond.* New York: Cambridge University Press, 1996.

Neal, Larry. "Black Writers Speak Out: A Symposium." *Negro Digest,* January 1968, 83–84.

Neal, Larry. "And Shine Swam On." In *Black Fire: An Anthology of Afro-American Writing,* ed. LeRoi Jones and Larry Neal, 638–56. New York: William Morrow, 1968.

New Jack City. Dir. Mario Van Peebles. 1991; Warner Home Video, 1998. DVD.

Nowatzki, Robert C. "'Our Only True National Poets': Blackface Minstrelsy and Cultural Nationalism." *American Transcendental Quarterly* 20, no. 1 (2006): 361–78.

Olson, Alix. "Diary of a Slam Poet." *Ms.,* December–January 2000, 66–73.

Ong, Walter J. *Orality and Literature: The Technologizing of the Word.* New York: Methuen, 1982.

Ortiz, Amalia. "Chicana Poet." E-mail communication, August 2, 2007.

Oxford English Dictionary. 2nd ed. Oxford: Oxford University Press, 1989.

Pareles, Jon. "A New Platform for the New Poets." *New York Times,* late ed., November 10, 2002, B1.

Paris Is Burning. Dir. Jennie Livingston. 1990; Off White Productions/Miramax, 2005. DVD.

Parker, Andrew, and Eve Kosofsky Sedgwick. "Introduction." In *Performativity and Performance,* ed. Andrew Parker and Eve Kosofsky Sedgwick, 1–18. New York: Routledge, 1995.

Parry, Albert. *Garrets and Pretenders: A History of Bohemianism in America.* New York: Dover, 1960.

Perry, Imani. *Prophets of the Hood: Politics and Poetics in Hip Hop.* Durham: Duke University Press, 2004.

"Poetry in Motion: Slam Dunking with Words." *Wall Street Journal,* September 10, 1998, A20.

Quickley, Jerry. "Hip Hop Poetry." In *Spoken Word Revolution: Slam, Hip Hop, and the Poetry of a New Generation,* ed. Mark Eleveld, 38–42. Naperville, IL: Sourcebooks MediaFusion, 2003.

"Release Dates for *Slam.*" Internet Movie Database, http://us.imdb.com/ReleaseDates?0139615 (accessed February 9, 2003).

Renee, Sonya. "THICK." In *Spoken Word Revolution Redux,* ed. Mark Eleveld, 10–11. Naperville, IL: Sourcebooks MediaFusion, 2007.

Rice, Edward Le Roy. *Monarchs of Minstrelsy: From "Daddy" Rice to Date.* New York: Kenny, 1911.

Russell Simmons Presents Def Poetry. Season 1, episode 1. 2002; HBO Video, 2004. DVD.

Russell Simmons Presents Def Poetry. Season 1, episode 3. 2002; HBO Video, 2004. DVD.

Russell Simmons Presents Def Poetry. Season 2, episode 2. 2003; HBO Video, 2005. DVD.

Richards, Jeremy. "Redeeming the Spectacle: Poetry Slams and the Informed Judges Proposal." In *Poems from the Big Muddy: The 2004 National Poetry Slam Anthology,* ed. Cristin O'Keefe Aptowicz, Jeremy Richards, and Scott Woods, 78–83. Whitmore Lake, MI: Wordsmith Press, 2004.

Robinson, Amy. "Forms of Appearance Value: Homer Plessy and the Politics of Privacy." In *Performance and Cultural Politics,* ed. Elin Diamond, 237–61. New York: Routledge, 1996.

Rodriguez, Luis J. "Crossing Boundaries, Crossing Cultures: Poetry, Performance, and the New American Revolution." *Another Chicago Magazine* 32–33 (spring–summer 1997): 46–50.

Rose, Tricia. *Black Noise: Rap Music and Black Culture in Contemporary America.* Music/Culture Series. Middletown, CT: Wesleyan University Press, 1994.

Ross, Andrew. *No Respect: Intellectuals and Popular Culture.* New York: Routledge, 1989.

Rudolph, Eric. "Shooting in the Big House: Documentary Techniques and Location Work Add Realism to the Prison Drama *Slam.*" *American Cinematographer* 79, no. 2 (1998): 116–17.

Samuels, David. "The Rap on Rap: The 'Black Music' That Isn't Either." *New Republic,* November 11, 1991, 24–29.

Seasholtz, Shappy. "I Am That Nerd." In *Spoken Nerd,* 1–2. New York: Little Vanity, 2002.

Sia, Beau. "An Open Letter to the Entertainment Industry." E-mail communication, June 24, 2007.

Silliman, Ron. "Who Speaks?: Ventriloquism and the Self in the Poetry Reading." In *Close Listening: Poetry and the Performed Word,* ed. Charles Bernstein, 360–78. New York: Oxford University Press, 1998.

Simmons, Danny, ed. *Russell Simmons Def Poetry Jam on Broadway . . . and More: The Choice Collection.* New York: Atria, 2003.

Slam. Dir. Marc Levin.1998; Trimark/Lions Gate, 1999. DVD.

Slamnation. Dir. Paul Devlin. 1998; Slammin' Entertainment, 2004. DVD.

Slam Planet: War of the Words. Dir. Mike Henry and Kyle Fuller. 2006; Slam Channel, 2006.

Smethurst, James. "'Pat Your Foot and Turn the Corner': Amiri Baraka, the Black Arts Movement, and the Poetics of a Popular Avant-Garde." *African American Review* 37, nos. 2–3 (2003): 261–70.

Smith, Marc. "About Slam Poetry." In *Spoken Word Revolution: Slam, Hip-Hop, and the Poetry of a New Generation,* ed. Mark Eleveld, 116–20. Naperville, IL: Sourcebooks MediaFusion, 2003.

Smith, Marc. Interview conducted at the 2002 National Poetry Slam, Minneapolis, by Susan B. A. Somers-Willett, August 16, 2002.

Smith, Marc. "Slam Info: Philosophies." http://www.slampapi.com/new_site/background/philosophies.htm (accessed February 25, 2003).

Smith, Marc, and Joe Kraynak. *The Complete Idiot's Guide to Slam Poetry.* New York: Alpha, 2004.

Smith, Patricia. *Big Towns, Big Talk.* Cambridge, MA: Zoland, 1992.

Smith, Patricia. "Persona Poem." In *Poetry Slam: The Competitive Art of Performance Poetry,* ed. Gary Mex Glazner, 70–75. San Francisco: Manic D Press, 2000.

Solis, Danny. "Aesthetics and Strategy of the Poetry Slam." In *Poetry Slam: The Competitive Art of Performance Poetry,* ed. Gary Mex Glazner, 88–93. San Francisco: Manic D Press, 2000.

Sollors, Werner. *Amiri Baraka/LeRoi Jones: The Quest for a "Populist Modernism."* New York: Columbia University Press, 1978.

Somers-Willett, Susan B. A. "Can Slam Poetry Matter?" *RATTLE* 13, no. 1 (2007): 85–90.

Somers-Willett, Susan B. A. "Def Poetry's Public: Spoken Word Poetry and the Racial Politics of Going Mainstream." *Iowa Journal of Cultural Studies* 8–9 (2006): 72–89.

Somers-Willett, Susan B. A. "Slam Poetry and the Cultural Politics of Performing Identity." *Journal of the Midwestern Modern Language Association* 38, no. 1 (2005): 51–73.

Spivak, Gayatri Chakravorty. "Can the Subaltern Speak?" In *Colonial Discourse and Post-colonial Theory: A Reader,* ed. Patrick Williams and Laura Chrisman, 66–111. New York: Harvester Wheatsheaf, 1993.

Stewart, James. "The Development of the Black Revolutionary Artist." In *Black Fire: An Anthology of Afro-American Writing,* ed. LeRoi Jones and Larry Neal, 3–10. New York: William Morrow, 1968.

Straight Out of Brooklyn. Dir. Matty Rich. 1991; Samuel Goldwyn/MGM, 2003. DVD.

Sullivan, James. "Uplifting Hip-Hop Show Really Tells It Like It Is: Well-Versed Poets Are Funny and Earthy in 'Def Poetry Jam'." *San Francisco Chronicle,* June 27, 2002, D1.

Tate, Greg, ed. *Everything But the Burden: What White People Are Taking from Black Culture.* New York: Broadway Books, 2003.

Tate, Greg, Grysha Coleman, Gary Dauphin, Arthur Jafa, Daniel Jones, Tamar Kali, Jimmy Lee, Vernon Reid, and Carl Hancock Rux. "Fade to Black." *Village Voice,* December 15, 1998, 152.

Taylor, Henry. "Read by the Author: Some Notes on Poetry in Performance." *Another Chicago Magazine* 32–33 (spring–summer 1997): 25–35.

Thomas, Lorenzo. "Neon Griot: The Function of Poetry Readings in the Black Arts Movement." In *Close Listening: Poetry and the Performed Word,* ed. Charles Bernstein, 300–323. New York: Oxford University Press, 1998.

Tillinghast, Richard. "American Poetry: Home Thoughts from Abroad." *Writer's Chronicle* 25, no. 5 (March–April 1993): 23–24.

Turner, Victor. *The Anthropology of Performance.* New York: Performing Arts Journal Publications, 1987.

The 2000 National Poetry Slam Finals. Poetry Slam, Incorporated, and Wordsmith Press, 2001. DVD.

Van Cleve, Genevieve. "I Was the Worst Feminist in the World." In *Gas, Food, Lodging, Poetry: Poems by the 1997 Austin Slam Team,* 26–27. Austin: Gaslight Productions, 1997.

Van Cleve, Genevieve. "Re: Slam." E-mail communication, October 30, 2001.

Watkins, S. Craig. *Hip Hop Matters: Politics, Pop Culture, and the Struggle for the Soul of a Movement.* Boston: Beacon, 2005.

Watkins, S. Craig. *Representing: Hip Hop Culture and the Production of Black Cinema.* Chicago: University of Chicago Press, 1998.

Whitman, Walt. "Ventures on an Old Theme." In *Prose Works.* Reprint; Bartleby.com, [1892] 2000. www.bartleby.com/229/3003.html.

"Who's Who in the Cast: Def Poetry Jam." *Playbill Theater Edition,* January 2003. Insert.

Williams, Saul. "Amethyst Rocks." In *Spoken Word Revolution: Slam, Hip-Hop, and the Poetry of a New Generation,* ed. Mark Eleveld, 55–57. Naperville, IL: Sourcebooks MediaFusion, 2003.

Williams, Saul. *The Dead Emcee Scrolls: The Lost Teachings of Hip-Hop.* New York: MTV/Pocket Books, 2006.

World's Greatest Poetry Slam, 2002. Poetry Slam, Incorporated, and Wordsmith Press, 2003. DVD.

Zumthor, Paul. *Oral Poetry: An Introduction.* Minneapolis: University of Minnesota Press, 1990.

Index

academic culture, 39–43. *See also* academic poetry; official verse culture

academic poetry: caricatures of, 41–42; public versus private issues, 40; tension with popular poetry, 22, 39–43

academic poetry readings, 3

academic verse. *See* academic poetry

Academy of American Poets, 2

African American identity. *See* marginalized identity; performances of blackness

"Age of Anxiety, The" (W. H. Auden), 54

AIDS crisis, 27

Algarín, Miguel, 137

American Idol, 136

American popular culture, 8, 12, 14, 39–43

"Amethyst Rocks" (Saul Williams), 33, 110, 128

Andrews, Sekou. *See* Sekou tha Misfit

antiracist identity, 85

antiwhite sentiment, 58, 59–60, 64–65, 102

Aptowicz, Cristin O'Keefe, 69, 154n23

argumentation and slam poetry, 26

Ashe, Krystal, 79

Association of Writers and Writing Programs, 1

Atlantic, 1

attitude of resistance: in Beat movement, 53–57; in Black Arts movement, 57–67; in blackface minstrelsy, 43, 48–49; in Def Poetry projects, 123; in popular poetry, 40–42, 66–67, 134; in slam poetry, 79, 134; in spoken word poetry, 132–33

Auden, W. H., 54

audience-as-critic, 5, 6, 20–21, 24, 134

Austin, J. L., 74, 109

authenticity: American popular culture and, 38; Beat movement and, 57, 66; Black Arts movement and, 66; black criminality and, 102; black identity and, 96–133; blackface minstrelsy and, 48, 66; connection with audience, 23; constructed nature of, 70, 161n3; criterion for success at poetry slams, 70–71; definition of, 73, 161n3; *Def Poetry* projects and, 114–28; gender identity and, 75, 99; hip-hop and, 12, 101–5; identity and, 8; identity poem and, 70–73; marginalized identity and, 76–86, 94; performance and, 8, 70; race and illusion of, 98–99, 110, 113, 129, 133; results of, 70, 161n3; self and, 73–76; in *Slam,* 105–14; slam poetry and, 7–8, 12, 36–39, 76–86, 92, 134; soul and, 57. *See also* realness

author: embodiment of, 17–18, 20, 69–71, 93; as performer, 32–33. *See also* authorship

authorship: embodiment and, 17–18, 20, 69–71, 93; hyperawareness of, 9, 33; performances of, 18, 19–20, 32–38, 68; rules of poetry